BUILDING BRIDGES

My lifelong journey to help heal a broken world

David Joseph

As told to Deborah Fineblum

Cover photo:
Peace Corps 1970 - 1972
Early days of bridge building -
me and a local friend in the village of Tessaoua, Niger

Table   of   Contents

"Dialogue is not just a technique. It's a way of life."
— Dave Joseph

FOREWORD
By Robert Stains, Jr.

I first met Dave at the annual meeting of the New England Society for Professionals in Dispute Resolution in the Summer of 1995. Part of my gig that year was to introduce what was then the "Public Conversations Project approach to dialogue" and get recruits for our first abortion dialogue facilitator training. The topic was on everyone's mind that year, in the wake of the abortion clinic shootings. People were scared and wanting to talk. I remember that Dave and I chatted a bit afterwards and I soon learned he'd applied to take the facilitator training that fall. Faced with a pool of fifty applicants, we ended up interviewing just thirteen for the six spots.

During our interview with Dave, as soon as he started speaking, I looked at Laura (that's therapist Laura Rockefeller Chasin who founded the Public Conversations Project, now Essential Partners) and she looked back at me and our eyes said, "This guy is awesome! We want this guy!!" He was savvy about group dynamics—but what we were feeling was more about Dave the man. How he held himself, how he interacted: he simply had no need to put himself forward, to be the expert or the smartest guy in the room. At the end of the interview when I found out that, like me, Dave was from Buffalo (and my high school to boot) I figured he must be, as my Dad used to describe very few men, "a stand-up guy:" smart, feet-on-the-ground, empathetic, and practical - a guy who would keep his word and do what he said he'd do. Dave was all that. We saw it that day and we would see it over and over again in the years to come.

Dave shone all through the rigorous training: six intense sessions over four months; five co-facilitations of some pretty heated abortion dialogues, videotaped as well as observed by us and other trainees through the one-way mirror after which the facilitators received feedback. You had to be really good to withstand this pressure, and Dave was, of course, the best. A true master: empathetic, unflappable in the face of challenge. We fell ever more deeply in love with him and wanted him on the team. After the training I kept in touch with him for years, always trying to find a way to bring him on at Public Conversations but we never had the funding. Until 2004, when Laura started the Leadership Fund, which was essentially at that time the Dave Fund, to bring him aboard.

Working with Dave was a complete delight; among other things, he was committed to a side-by-side approach that started with curiosity and was marked by connected communication. And if you worked with Dave, you knew that he cared about you and would always have your back.

Dave was steady and unflappable in the face of trouble. Trouble visited us when we worked on a project together with high stakes:

its success or failure would have huge implications for thousands of people. After working with a deeply divided team in two separate groups over the space of seven months, the time came to bring the groups together for an actual dialogue. The Friday before the scheduled Monday dialogue, one of the participants sent an email to all the others urging them to cancel the dialogue and end the project, saying that Dave and I were not to be trusted because of our backgrounds as therapists. After seven months of work, we were alarmed. In those moments when we scrambled to figure out how to respond, Dave exhibited two of his greatest qualities: steadfastness and a willingness to "trust the group." Rather than respond with advocacy or defensiveness, Dave's reaction was for us to simply say to the group, "Let us know what you decide."

I'm convinced that his restraint that day was the hinge-moment in that work. Once people saw that we were not going to force the issue, they decided to move forward into one of the most powerful dialogues that either of us had ever been part of.

As one of the top pros in the field of conflict transformation, Dave taught thousands of people in the United States and around the world many of the secrets of peaceful coexistence through the arts of mediation and Reflective Structured Dialogue. But the teaching that stands out the most in my mind — that had the biggest effect on our thinking at Public Conversations—was that "Dialogue is not just a technique. It's a way of life." And, as Dave loved to say, "It's only good for those of us who have to deal with other human beings." This thinking deeply reflects his commitment to *tikkun olam*, Hebrew for "repair of the world", a concept we first learned from him back in 1996 during the training finale wrap-up.

Dave played Bill Staines' song "Bridges" that night. That song said everything about Dave's personal commitment to *tikkun olam*, and everything about how those of us privileged to know and love him felt about him.

> *There are bridges, bridges in the sky*
> *They are shining in the sun*
> *They are stone and steel and wood and wire*
> *They can change two things to one.*
>
> *They are languages and letters*
> *They are poetry and awe*
> *They are love and understanding*
> *And they're better than a wall.*
> *There are canyons, there are canyons*
> *They are yawning in the night*
> *They are rank and bitter anger*
> *And they are all devoid of light.*

They are fear and blind suspicion

They are apathy and pride

They are dark and so foreboding

And they're oh, so very wide.

Let us build a bridge of music

Let us cross it with a song

Let us span another canyon

Let us right another wrong.

Oh, and if someone should ask us

Where we are bound today

We will tell them, "Building Bridges"

And be off and on our way.

Robert R. Stains, Jr. runs Bob Stains and Associates,
specializing in conflict transformation,
and is Senior Associate at Essential Partners.

Song "Bridges" reprinted with permission from Bill Staines.

7

INTRODUCTION
By Andrea Joseph

It's miraculous that this book ever got off the ground, to say nothing of the fact that it has been published. That's because the author suffered a recurrence of Glioblastoma Multiforme (GBM), a terminal brain tumor, in October of 2020. It was a labor of love for David to begin it when he knew he was dying, and it became my labor of love to complete it for him after he died one year later.

This is how it came to pass. At some point following the recurrence, David re-connected with the hospital chaplain he had met while he was awaiting surgery for the GBM back in 2016. He and Rabbi Natan Schafer had immediately formed a close bond that lasted well beyond the hospital stay. Although he had since moved to Israel, Rabbi Schafer, during calls that were scheduled to accommodate the time difference, urged David to write a memoir and tell his story. David resisted. He protested that he wasn't interested in a vanity project, and he really didn't enjoy writing. But the Rabbi persisted, making the case for a memoir that could be of value for others in the field of dialogue and peacebuilding and he recommended Deborah Fineblum, a ghostwriter he knew who could take on the task of getting David's story committed to paper. David relented.

And so, this memoir was born....

Although failing physically and mentally, David went on to have multiple conversations with Deborah, from which she was able to construct a coherent manuscript that we hope will provide insights, inspiration and encouragement to its readers.

Ordinarily in the introduction the author acknowledges people who helped bring the book to fruition and takes responsibility for errors and omissions. Sadly, David is not here to do that, so that task falls to me. And there are so many people who took the time to make sure the information contained in this book is as accurate as possible. Bob Stains, John Sarrouf, Prahba Sankarnaranayan, Ginny Morrison, Raye Rawls, and Steve Seeche provided background material and took time to talk with Deborah so she would have as deep an understanding as a newbie to the field could have, in addition to some critical facts. Alison Baron filled me in on several projects. Seth Karamage, David's self-described and beloved African son, kept David abreast of developments in the project they had started in Nigeria just before Covid interrupted. If I have omitted mentioning anyone who should have been acknowledged, or if there are factual errors, please accept my most sincere apology.

Despite the recurrence of his illness, David remained true to form. Yes, he was scared, but he chose to continue to live as fully as possible, doing what he loved to do: spending time with his family, staying in touch with colleagues at Essential Partners and friends via Zoom, continuing in his role as President of the board of Mediators Beyond Borders International, and mentoring his young colleagues.

There is no one on earth whose story David wouldn't want to hear, or who he didn't think deserved the full support of family, community, and the state systems in which they lived. The way he led his life reflected the true man. During his seventy-three years, the way we've come to understand and clarify language that deals with identity and challenging issues has evolved, and, while prior to his final illness he gladly adopted new terms, the way he expressed certain ideas while dictating for this book may reflect the terminology used at an earlier time. Our family hopes that readers will consider his words with the same generosity of spirit with which he offered them in this memoir and offered them by the way he lived every day.

CHAPTER 1
MY FORMATIVE YEARS:
CHILDHOOD THROUGH COLLEGE

My dad, Donald Alfred Joseph, was a Buffalonian born and bred, and so am I. He met my mom, Dvorah (née Sperling), while he was stationed in Birmingham, Alabama (her hometown) during World War II. They married when he returned from the war and settled in Buffalo. By the time I was born on July 23, 1948, my dad was already a high school history teacher. My younger sister Judy was born in 1950, and Ruthie three years later. Dad went on to earn his MA and was a much-loved elementary school principal for the rest of his career.

My mom was home with us until I was starting high school, when she went back to school for her MSW. She was dedicated to alleviating the pain of poverty. She worked for Planned Parenthood for many years, and also as a housing advocate. She was a profound influence on my thinking as I grew up.

I'm the oldest of three, but I grew up feeling like I was one of ten. My dad's brother Norman married Shirley Troyan and they had three kids. Shirley's sister Marion and her husband Dick Connuck had four kids. They lived a little further out, but it felt then, and still feels today, like we were one big family. Only when I was in college did I realize that we weren't directly related to our cousins' cousins.

My parents were observant Conservative Jews, very active in their congregation. My mom taught Saturday (not Sunday) school, and my dad was President of the board for many years. I grew up secure within the small but active Jewish community of greater Buffalo. When the Jews began moving out of the city, Kenmore was the first stop, and that's where we lived until I went off to college. Our neighborhood had lots of kids of all stripes, and we all got along well. During the winter, some of the fathers would ice over their backyards and we would play ice hockey or just skate. We did that in our backyard too. Another benefit of living there was that the town ran a sort of summer camp with sports. That's where I learned to play tennis and developed a lifelong love of the sport.

Since my dad's parents lived just a few miles away, we often had Shabbat dinner at Grandma and Grandpa's. I can still see the roast beef coming out of the oven and the string Grandma used to bind it together. I can also see Grandma and Grandpa at the head of the table, my dad to my right and my mom to my left. My dad's brother and his wife and kids are often there too. There's a very warm, very happy feeling in the room, as there was at all the shared holidays, whether at my grandparents', our home or one of the cousin's homes. As an adult, I recognize that there must have been conflicts or tensions at times, as there are in all families, but they were never serious enough to have influenced my memories in any negative way. My beloved grandfather's unexpected death just three months before my Bar Mitzvah was very upsetting. That trauma followed me into adulthood and I remember experiencing anxiety that I would face a similar loss in the months leading up to my wedding. Thankfully, no such thing happened.

My mom's father in Birmingham, Alabama was known as a rabbi's rabbi — a Biblical and Talmudic scholar. Though not an official rabbi, he was the one the rabbis went to with their questions. *Zeyde* (Yiddish for grandfather) sold insurance to get by, but teaching Torah was his love. My maternal grandmother died when I was still quite young; I don't have solid memories of her, and for reasons of her own, my mother did not talk about her very much. My mother's brother remained in Birmingham, along with many other family members, and to this day there is a large annual family reunion barbeque every summer.

My mother was so uncomfortable with the situation for black people in the south that we only went once to Birmingham (and that was not until after the Civil Rights Bill passed) to visit my *Zeyde* and attend the reunion. But he visited us every summer. I remember his whiskers, and the warm feeling I always had toward him. But the idea of summer in Birmingham with relatives I did not know very well held less appeal as I grew older, and I never attended the reunion after that one family trip.

Because I saw so many examples of educators in my family — my dad as a school principal and former teacher, my mom an informal Jewish educator and my *Zeyde* teaching Jewish thought — I always imagined I'd go into teaching too. Ultimately, that's what I did do, in my own way.

But I also thought maybe I'd be a lawyer. Watching Perry Mason, and preoccupied from an early age with the idea of right and wrong, I was attracted to the law. Later, I began to see mediation and dialogue as a better way for people to gain access to justice; the idea of defending people as a lawyer slowly gave way to helping them have access to justice without having to involve the courts.

In school I excelled at the subjects I enjoyed; history, social studies, science, and math all interested me. But even though I was particularly good at those subjects, I never thought of going into those fields.

I learned that we can help someone think through their problems and ask themselves, "Is there a way to be heard, to have my rights recognized, without having to go through the painful — and often very expensive — legal system?" The same principle, I began to see as I got more experience, works with families and communities. And it starts, I would soon learn, with improving communication.

In school, I was greatly influenced by one special teacher. Ida Fabian came into my life in ninth or tenth grade. She taught social studies in a highly unorthodox way. Miss Fabian was bright and well-spoken. By asking great questions, she stimulated us to think about things we'd never thought about before: Was North America "discovered" by Europeans? When the white man arrived, did he drive up the Mass Pike from Boston? How does what really happened relate to what's written in history books? And, just as important, she encouraged us to ask questions. She expected a lot of us: to examine the facts we were being taught, to integrate them

14

and to consider how they relate to each other. In many ways Miss Fabian was my first role model of what a teacher could be, what a teacher should be, and the way just one teacher can influence a kid's entire future for the better. She certainly did that for me.

The other teacher who helped lead me on the path I would eventually follow was closer to home: my mother, who never had a shortage of books, and who taught me to understand family and group dynamics. She also taught me to see how the adults that black and white kids grow up with — in such different and unequal environments, and with such different expectations, especially in school — result in different, usually predictable, outcomes.

It was my mother who taught me how important it is to have someone in a kid's life with high expectations for them, to teach them never to accept failure as a given and help them to succeed without lowering the standards.

I had an early opportunity to see these principles applied in our neighborhood school. We had kids from low-income families, and others from families who were better off, solidly blue-collar or middle class. A good number of our graduates went on to college. But not unexpectedly, these were kids who came from more affluent families.

During my teen years my dad and I used to get into serious discussions - sometimes heated disagreements - about what was going on in the world during that tumultuous '60s decade. He had been a history teacher for many years and was well informed, but he was generally a more conservative Democrat than I or my mother. By high school, I was feeling frustrated with the slow pace of racial and social change, while my father felt things would change in their own good time.

As I mentioned, my mother was a huge influence on my emerging commitment to social justice. She had grown up with a strong father figure who encouraged her studies. But also as a southern girl, even one whose family was not especially well off, she was raised in part by a black woman, a nanny, who took care of her and her brother. The nanny had given the care of her own son into the hands of others so she could earn enough to support them. When at an early age my mother came to understand what this meant, she became extremely sensitive to the living conditions of the black families in Birmingham. She always had a personal face — her nanny's — to put on the struggle for equal rights and opportunity. I have a memory of her travelling to Washington D.C. to march in some of the big civil rights demonstrations. My memory may not be accurate, but I know that's where her very strong sympathies lay.

My own commitment to the civil rights movement and social change only grew stronger during my college years. I went to Harpur College in Binghamton, NY; in 1965 it became one of the four state universities, although for a time it was still known as Harpur. As SUNY Binghamton its student body grew quickly from 2,500 when I entered in 1966, to 5,000 by the time I left in 1970 – the impact of the baby boom hitting our college years.

At school, majoring in philosophy was an easy choice for me. I remember thinking the subject was actually practical, because philosophers reflected on questions like what life is all about, and what makes life worth living — ethics in general, you might say. These are the things I was already thinking about every day, and now I could take classes on them every day: what could be better? I liked to joke that as soon as I graduated with this degree I'd apply for the first philosopher king position that came along.

I came in sideways to psychotherapy, which captured my interest once I got involved with Upward Bound. When I first heard about Upward Bound, I thought, here was something I can do that would be of service.

Upward Bound provides support to participants in their preparation for college entrance. The program gives opportunities to students to succeed in their pre-college performance and ultimately in higher education. These high school students from low-income families often represent their families' first generation to attain a degree in higher education.

In my sophomore and junior years, I was an on-campus tutor and mentor during the school year, and a counselor for the program in the summers. It was exciting! I enjoyed working with the kids, and it felt like a way to be involved in and make a real contribution to the civil rights movement.

My experience with Upward Bound pointed me in the direction of my future career. It got me thinking about how much I liked working with adolescents in a couple of different capacities:

as a teacher, and as someone to be there to show them a path to their aspirations. With the civil rights movement in the air, the possibility of helping pull kids up out of poverty into the opportunities America had to offer was a powerful force.

Around that time, Arthur Ashe began to win tennis tournaments and his name was in the news. He was a groundbreaker, a black man who dared to succeed in a white man's sport. As a tennis player myself in both high school and college, I was more than several levels below him, but it was clear that he had the athletic talent to get to the top. What he did at that moment in history took a great deal of personal courage and confidence. It also took some generosity on the part of the white people who let him in the door to the tennis world — traditionally a white, middle and upper class sport. Still, Ashe had an uphill fight to get where he was, eventually becoming the Jackie Robinson of tennis. For me and my Upward Bound kids, Ashe was an inspiration, showing us what's possible.

In my last year of college, I started thinking about what I wanted to do afterward. It came down to two options: working for VISTA to help poor people in the US, or joining the Peace Corps. I applied to both. When I got home from spring vacation, I found two letters in the mailbox: one from Vista, which offered work with Native Americans, and the other from the Peace Corps, offering me the chance to teach English in French-speaking Africa. I didn't want to look back and say I'd passed up the only chance I'd ever have to go to Africa, so I decided that it had to be the Peace Corps.

I didn't realize it then, but I was on my way to my first major life-changing experience.

18

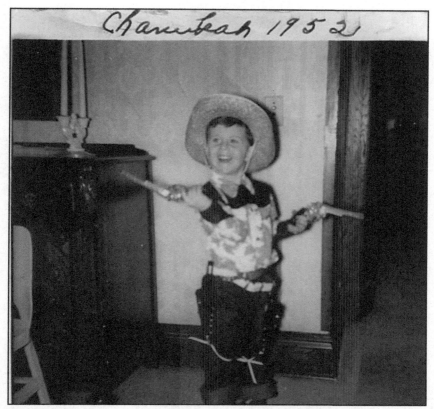

Chanukah 1952

Judy, me, and Ruthie

19

"So you think she's gonna say yes?"

Our wedding, May 25, 1975

20

May 25, 1975: Our Wedding Day
L-R Joel Bender, my bride Andrea Bender Joseph, me, Sylvia Joseph,
Don Joseph, Dvorah Joseph, Shirley Bender, Sam Bender

Buffalo, 1977: L – R Dvorah (Bubba Dee) Joseph,
Don Joseph (Grandpa), Sylvia Joseph (great grandmother),
Andrea, and me holding our first born son, Jesse

Alaska, 2002: Seth, Jesse, Andrea, me

Pilansberg, South Africa 2017: self-driving safari:
L-R Seth, me, Andrea, Alex, Jesse (wildebeests in background)

Cuba, January 2020: L-R Andrea, me, sister Judy Ramsey,
Bruce Ramsey, sister Ruth Ma'ayan, Dick Fate

Super Bowl 2017!

Lincoln, RI circa 2016:
Reading with my grandkids Alex, Stella, and Pierce.
(The 4th and final, Davey, had yet to make his appearance.)

Disney World, FL 2020:
The Joseph gang's all here L-R Front - Jodie, Seth, Davey, Jesse
Back – Stella, Pierce, Alex, me, Andrea

Sare, France, 2020:
Happily officiating
as Sara Jacobs becomes the bride of Araud Sehabiague.
Bottom left corner - proud dad Marc Jacobs sitting next to younger
daughter Alisa watching.

I also officiated at both my sisters' weddings
and that of our godson Joshua Peckins between 2016-2020.

CHAPTER 2
BEGINNING MY PATH:
LEARNING TO TEACH WITH LOVE

So I accepted the Peace Corps' offer. After graduation, I headed for the village of Tessaoua in Niger. I would live for two years (1970-1972) in this town of 5,000 at the southern edge of the Sahara Desert. My assignment was to teach English to high school students as their third language. They already knew Hausa, their indigenous tongue, as well as French, which was both the official and "street" language in which their families did business.

This experience was going to shape the rest of my life, not just because I learned the basics of teaching something that was totally foreign to the kids, but also because I learned how not to teach, how not to treat people. It was the beginning of what would become my understanding of the fundamental principles behind dialogue and mediation.

I learned that I love to teach. We did crazy things like acting out plays, singing songs, writing letters to soul singer James Brown (whom they knew and adored). The point was to find any and all ways for the kids to use this strange new language as a means of communication.

My teaching methods were considered a bit unorthodox. As a former French colony, Niger had an education system based on the traditional French model: listen, take notes, then regurgitate. The headmaster used to ask me what was wrong with my classes. He was less interested in what was wrong with my classes, however, than whether our students could do well on the standardized tests. If they performed well, it would reflect honor on him and his high school. Eventually, when I asked him if this was his primary concern and he said yes, I told him, "I guarantee you, if you let me continue with my crazy teaching, they will do better next year. It's going to happen." He smiled and said, "It'd better happen." Fortunately, it did.

As I was teaching English, I myself was learning French. In fact, I managed to learn it well enough to impress the Parisians on a trip Andrea and I took thirty years later, in 2003. I was mistaken on that trip for a Frenchman—not just any Frenchman but Lionel Jospin, the former prime minister! While there is a strong physical resemblance, this was still a high compliment on my language skills for a kid from Buffalo.

So, my first job was being paid (very modestly) by the US government to teach kids in West Africa to speak English as a third language. I quickly realized that this couldn't be done by teaching the kids in French, which was a second language for most. Their first language was Hausa, in which they communicated for most of their days (and evenings).

The most important thing I learned was that this new foreign language would need to be taught in a way that was adapted to their lives. In other words, the English I'd be teaching needed to reflect what was happening in their day-to-day lives as students living in that place at that time. They needed to be able to express life on their family's farms, in their school, with their friends. Needless to say, African teens lead different lives than their French peers, and they need a very different vocabulary than that of their French textbooks to express themselves.

I was inspired to create such a program for them, and in many ways had the *chutzpa* (Yiddish for "nerve") to teach it, largely thanks to the work of Arthur John Spring. Arthur was an expert language teacher for the Peace Corps who trained those of us who would be teaching English. He taught me that when you're teaching, you need to teach to feelings as much as to the students' minds. If you don't know (and basically if you're not interested in) your students' lives — what they laugh about, what they care about, what they might be afraid of — teaching them is going to be a lot more difficult.

In order to teach to feelings, you must be willing to learn as much as you can about your students' culture and the details of their lives. And, as you connect with them, imagine that the shoe is on the other foot — that you are the one who's learning something entirely new, and they are responsible for educating you. That openness to seeing students as our teachers lies at the heart of what Arthur taught us, and at the heart of what I really needed to learn. When I made it my job to ask about their lives, and to see our students as also our teachers, I learned that I was then greeted with an openness and receptivity to what I was there to teach them.

But again, the rigid French system was still not receptive to this approach. Even though I loved teaching, I wasn't happy trying to teach these kids within that system, and it violated my sense of their human dignity. So, as my time in the Peace Corps drew to a close, I began to look for a place where I could teach the way I had discovered actually works, a way that gives the students the respect they deserve and the experience of loving to learn.

BACK TO AMERICA

After those years of fighting a system so resistant to change, so insistent on "teaching to the test," I knew I needed to work in a school where I could be free to use, experiment with, and develop new ways of learning in order to truly connect with and inspire the next generation.

In 1972, just back from Africa, I found a place that not only allowed this, it encouraged it: Murray Road, an alternative high school in Newton, Massachusetts. The school was looking for someone to teach immersion French, photography, and philosophy — basically, whatever subjects the kids were interested in learning. I was hired as a teaching assistant (that's all they had in the budget), but given the freedom and responsibilities of a full-fledged teacher.

Murray Road granted me the freedom to teach experientially. I would often take classes to downtown Boston to take pictures, and then we'd return to school and develop them in the school darkroom. In one course called "No More Lies," about American history, we'd compare standard American history textbooks to see how differently they framed events in history. It was eye-opening for the kids, and for me, too.

The job gave me an opportunity to really get to know these kids. Many of them came to talk about their problems, maybe because I was one of only two teachers under twenty-five and they felt I could relate to them. As with the tutoring and mentoring with Upward Bound when I was in college, I felt I could have a positive impact on those kids.

While teaching for two years in Newton, I lived in a communal house in nearby Watertown. I met Andrea, who was also teaching at that time (but who went on to have a fulfilling career in fundraising) through a summer job between school years. We were part of a small team of door-to-door sales people for Great Books of the Western World (a division of the Encyclopedia Britannica). Perhaps because we were both so unsuited to this kind of work, and certainly because we both had to contend with an unethical team leader who tried to cheat us out of the "guaranteed" salary, we bonded, and dated throughout my second year of teaching in Newton.

During that second year, I realized that as much as I loved teaching, I was making just $4,900 a year - low pay even in 1974. Andrea and I had started talking about marriage and having kids, so it was time to move on professionally. Plus I knew I'd have to take a master's degree if I ever hoped to be an agent for change and impact more people's lives.

But what should I study? The group that lived in our house included two social workers and a psychologist, and we often talked about how they were helping people. Those conversations, combined with my mother's influence, the enjoyment I experienced from my close relationships with my Newton students, and the one-on-one help I had given teens back in Upward Bound, meant that a master's degree in therapeutic social work began to sound right.

CHAPTER 3
A NEW DIRECTION:
GRADUATE SCHOOL
AND TAKING UP THE THERAPEUTIC LIFE

Looking back over more than a half century, I can see how these early experiences pointed to emerging possibilities that would only find expression years later. But every step — and misstep — brought me closer to a vision and understanding of ways to undertake the healing I dreamed to accomplish.

First it was my students, and for many years afterwards it would be my clients, who showed me how much the world needs the skills of peacemaking through constructive conversations and dialogue, and it was they who initially pointed me in the directions in which I needed to grow.

BACK TO SCHOOL

By 1974 I knew I had to get another degree to move forward in life. Based on how much I enjoyed helping adolescents through those traumatic years, focusing on the therapeutic aspect of social work made the most sense to me. But where could I find the kind of master's program that would take a creative and affirming approach to therapy that resembled the one that I'd found worked so well in the classroom?

The best fit I found was Smith College, in Western Massachusetts. It was a women's school, but the social work grad program was co-ed, and there were fifteen of us men in the class of fifty. Being in such a minority didn't bother me. I grew up with strong female models: a mother who was passionately committed to her beliefs and worked to promote them, and two very bright, hardworking, and caring sisters. Judy, the older of my sisters, began her professional life as a social worker and has carried those values throughout her career, and Ruthie is a physical therapist who is a caring and creative advocate for her patients. I have also lived with an intelligent, loving wife for more than four decades, and have enjoyed many strong relationships with women as some of my closest associates and partners over the years.

The social work program at Smith had an unorthodox schedule: three summers of academic courses, and internships during the typical school years in between. Meaning it was heavily weighted to the kind of experiential learning I thrived on. For my then-girlfriend Andrea (soon to be my wife), this was hard: I spent summers in what she jokingly called "summer camp in the Berkshires" surrounded by women, and the first year working long hours in a locked ward with some pretty disturbed patients.

I think making it through that experience laid the groundwork for our long-term success at marriage.

But the hands-on part of Smith's program proved excellent training for beginning to think like a therapist, whether in a one-on-one, couple, family, or group therapy setting. Looking back on the program, I can also see that the years I'd taught in both Africa and Newton, and even the Upward Bound tutoring I'd done in college, contributed great value to my education as a therapist, especially when it came to adolescents. Years later, both roles were mainstays of my work in dialogue, as the therapeutic and the educational began to fuse and grow into a system for creating genuine curiosity where previously there was only an assumption of knowing.

One enduring influence on me during graduate school was learning Thomas Gordon's "Parent Effectiveness Training," an approach that had as much to teach a new therapist as it did a parent — and I did make use of many of these principles when I became a parent. A program that had already stood the test of time for raising responsible children, PET taught me the concept of "reflexive listening": people (of all ages) are much more willing to listen to you if they feel heard. They have to know you're really committed to understanding their viewpoint and it has to be sincere. Kids especially can tell if you value what they're saying or if you're just humoring them. I already saw how well this worked in Africa and Newton but for me, Gordon showed it so clearly, down to the many applications that were highly reproducible in a wide variety of settings. (The PET book was first published in 1970 and is still available on Kindle and as an audiobook.)

Years later, when I supervised students who did the more traditional schedule of classes during the school year and internships in the summer, or split the day between the two activities, I came to appreciate even more how fortunate I had been to have such immersive graduate training. In a full-time placement you learn more, and you learn faster, too.

MY FIRST THERAPY JOB

Andrea and I married in the spring before my final summer at Smith. It was my first marriage, but Andrea's second — she'd been married (with pomp and circumstance) briefly to someone for whom marriage apparently exacerbated some issues that he refused to address. His loss was my gain! Andrea and I were very happy to have a small outdoor wedding at Saugus Ironworks in Saugus, Massachusetts. It's a National Historic Site, and far more wooded and idyllic than it sounds. Ours was the first wedding held there. A rabbi officiated and friends and family provided a pot-luck dinner. I remember that the day had started out overcast, but by the time we arrived at the site, the sun was shining and it was a beautiful, perfect day for us.

So, in 1975, as a newlywed just out of graduate school, I had to ask myself, what's the best way to put my MSW degree to work for the greater good? Since I'd focused on the therapeutic aspect of social work and not the casework side of the profession, I took a job as a psychotherapist at the Herb Lipton Mental Health Clinic, serving the communities around Ayer, northwest of Boston.

Though there were some wealthy families in the nearby town of Groton, which was included in our service area, most of the people living in the area were blue-collar or entry-level white-collar families. In that way it reminded me of the part of Buffalo where I was raised: a real mix economically, socially, and educationally. It's the kind of mix I've always valued and appreciated.

Most of my time at that clinic was spent working with individuals, with couples and also with the families of teens. I was able to specialize in working with teenagers, creating the rapport I'd felt beginning with my Upward Bound experience in college and which had grown stronger in my years of teaching both in Africa and in Newton.

What was great about that job was that I worked half-time as a psychotherapist and the other half as a psychiatric consultant to juvenile and adult courts and police departments. This experience was a bit different from that of my colleagues, who were strictly psychotherapists in a one-on-one setting. I got to hear from the police, the schools, the courts, the parents, and, of course, the kids. As a consultant, working with a juvenile court concerned with custody and with school systems, it was my first experience with helping opposing parties be able to see each other's point of view enough to work out the best solution for everyone, in this case starting with the teen.

As a teacher, I had enjoyed the informal contact with kids when they decided I was approachable. It allowed me to form a different kind of relationship with them. But now as a therapist and a court and police consultant, that rapport was funneled into a more formal way of relating, and I saw more clearly than ever before how different perspectives are shaped by our different early environment and experiences.

You talk to a teenager, and you think this poor kid has picked the short straw in the parents' lottery. Other times, you meet parents and think, "Oh my God, how did these two great people produce this kid?" I quickly learned that when you are in a position like mine, with so many voices telling you what's going on, you can have your own opinions but not your own facts. Facts are real and must be respected.

But in family therapy and in negotiating the best solution vis-à-vis the courts, the schools, and so on, the challenge is to both acknowledge the facts and also be able to bridge the gulf of the different perspectives in play. I found that one of the most underrated family therapy skills is listening to each side of the debate with an understanding that can help everyone put aside their positions long enough to see the other's side. This is often a slow process, and it takes a willingness on everyone's part to be open to an opposing view in what is often a heated situation involving a teen. But as I began to see at this job, it can be done and when it does happen, everyone wins, especially the kid. And a solution usually comes more easily with this openness than without it.

In those years I got to know these communities from multiple perspectives — the police, the teen, the parents, the schools — and this experience more than any other I'd had up to then helped me appreciate differences in upbringing and environment and how they affect our beliefs and the way we see the world and its challenges. It sensitized me to the fact that everyone has their own perspective and way of seeing the world and their part in it. I learned then that the wisest decisions come from creating an environment where people can listen to each other and together create a shared understanding, and that this is the only path to real peace. I also learned, between the courts, the police, the schools, the families, and the teens I worked with, how much more likely it is that each party will listen if they feel they've been listened to. That simple act creates a vulnerability that can uncover things that would never have been spoken otherwise. I could see clearly that, no matter what the disagreement was, people would feel more invested in finding a solution when you've created an environment that nurtures a safe place to work out problems. And you never know beforehand what conditions will be safe for everyone. You have to be able to be flexible enough to create that safe place anew with each problem that needs solving.

Years later I learned that mediation is similar to therapy in that everyone needs to tell their story and each person needs to feel heard, only in mediation they feel heard by the "other," not by the therapist. This takes an even greater leap into understanding "the other's" experience and beliefs. This awareness, which grew more fleshed-out during those years, would become part of everything I would do in the future.

It was during these years while I was at Ayer that our two sons were born, Jesse in 1977 and Seth three years later. And, even though it had been a good 10 years at Ayer I began to see that I had learned whatever I could there. That, and our growing family, motivated me to find a position where I would take on more responsibility.

So, in 1985 I took a supervisory position in LUK (Let Us Know) Crisis Center, a multi-service agency focused on teens dealing with drug addictions. My main responsibilities there were providing counseling and supervising other clinicians. But it was a rough match from the start. I didn't mind the long hours but almost from the beginning, I wrestled with significant differences I had with the administration.

I could see how much my stress was affecting Andrea and the boys, who were seven and ten when I took the job. I had committed to the administration that I would stay on for at least three years and really wanted to keep my word. But two years in, the effect on all of us was so clearly harmful that I had to make the decision that would be the best for my family, and I resigned.

Happily, a position as Director of Addiction and Mental Health Services at the Attleboro Mental Health Center in southern Massachusetts had opened up and I would spend a productive eight years there doing mostly family therapy and again supervising other therapists. I also worked with the police — training them in the best ways to deal with addiction issues — as well as with local organizations and clinicians providing addiction services.

In 1995, towards the end of those Attleboro years, I heard about an intensive four-month training program for volunteers to learn dialogue facilitation skills through the PCP, the Public Conversations Project (now known as Essential Partners). Once trained, we practioners would facilitate dialogues about a highly-charged subject — such as abortion. I applied and was accepted, which ultimately led to the next stage of my career.

Interestingly, those of us who were selected all had strong therapeutic backgrounds. We also knew the topic about which we would be facilitating was not going to be an easy one. It was the era of the abortion clinic shootings, and the issue was highly emotional for everyone on both sides of the divide. People were screaming at each other and calling each other terrible names. Laura Chasin, a family therapist working in Cambridge, MA, founded PCP with several other colleagues to apply principles of family therapy to enable people with strongly held beliefs on both sides of the abortion debate to have a safe space to learn about each other. The goal was not to change minds but, through structured dialogue, to help participants humanize "the other" and reduce the hateful polarization that was tearing families and communities apart.

It was challenging but fascinating work, facilitating some pretty heated sessions around abortion. Those months in the program not only introduced me to many of the principles, concepts, and skills I would be using for the next quarter century but also to some of the people I would eventually partner with on peace-making projects around the world.

At the time I was still working full-time at Attleboro and doing my best to partner with Andrea in raising our now teenage sons (she was also working full-time in nonprofit fundraising and our days were full).

It was at that time that I decided to take a risk and ventured into my first and only for-profit venture, starting a business with a friend and partner who had experience in hospital administration. It was still in the service sector but provided elder-care services. While the idea itself was a sound one and much-needed, unfortunately it was a concept ahead of its time. Making it work as a business was quite difficult and we ended up shutting it down after a few years of giving it our best.

While I would have loved to have gone to work at PCP then, the organization was not in a position to hire me at that point, but I remained active as a volunteer. My next position was in another therapeutic role, this one at the East Bay Mental Health Center in East Providence where, from 1998-2002, I carried a caseload and supervised clinicians. As always, teens and their families were a focus of mine.

Fortunately, awareness of the benefits of mediation was growing at the time and, while at East Bay, I helped get the Providence Community Mediation Center (now known as the Center for Mediation and Collaboration RI) off the ground as a founding board member.

The field was increasingly calling to me. From my first taste of the power of mediation and dialogue to open minds and hearts and diffuse some pretty explosive situations — remember I began with abortion at a very painful time — I was getting more and more excited about its potential, not only for the kind of therapeutic work I was doing and overseeing, but way beyond that, to every kind of conflict imaginable.

Throughout all these years of working in therapeutic settings I was increasingly aware of what wasn't working. These years of working with individuals, couples, and families served to sensitize me to the fact that so often what people seek help with is not the root of the real problem. And, whereas most people —including many therapists — focus on the content of the conflict, what I really enjoy is switching the focus to the relationship and the different ways people relate to relationship and to trust - a very different approach. So, I would often focus our conversations not only on the issues at hand but also on the way the parties relate to each other as contributing to the problem. I would ask them to reflect on how the issue on the table may reflect their deeper issues, issues that, once understood and addressed, could help them avoid future conflicts. This way they develop tools and skills to use when the need arises again.

I began to see that these principles of open empathetic communication work with every kind of conflict in every kind of relationship. Whether in marital or family, workplace, communal, religious, ethnic, or political situations, peace-making begins with the willingness to take a risk, to let down your guard long enough to truly see where the other person is coming from. Only then are people really open to working together on a solution. At this time I was becoming increasingly determined to create opportunities to think proactively and apply some of the values of mediation to the purpose of relationship-rescue, problem-solving, and rapport-building, for consistency.

I couldn't have known then how much the convergence of my therapeutic work with my mediation training would change my life path and direct me where I ultimately needed to go.

CHAPTER 4
THE RIGHT PERSON AT THE RIGHT TIME:
BUILDING THE ART OF PEACE

Working on the ground floor of the Providence Mediation Center, I began to see that, more than a science, there is an art to making peace, and it shares aspects of family therapy and mediation — as well as education — when they're done right. To succeed in any of these things, you have to practice deep, active listening: that is the first step to achieving peace. You have to demonstrate genuine interest in and respect for all participants. And you have to relate the dialogue to their life experiences and belief systems. Whether it's between family members, business partners, religious groups, or political parties, the principles remain exactly the same.

By 2002, the Providence center had been renamed the Rhode Island Community Mediation Center (it has since been renamed the Center for Mediation and Collaboration RI) and I was asked to be its Executive Director.

I saw the role as a golden opportunity to have a wider impact on the community, and beyond that, the state, in helping resolve all types of disputes.

But after two years of the day-to-day administrative tasks of running the agency, I realized that I missed working in the trenches, facilitating in a more direct-service way. Fortunately, an opportunity opened up at the Public Conversations Project, the Massachusetts-based organization I'd been active in for years, in the position of Program Director. Once I fully dove into the waters of dialogue and peace-making as a profession, things began to move quickly. And for the last two decades I've been able to do the kind of work that's been both my vocation and avocation, able to blend my passion and my skills in ways most people never get a chance to do.

This position presented a perfect way for me to work toward making the greatest impact for good; it involved plenty of direct facilitating, balanced by supervision and training. Over the next fifteen years I helped develop a process called Reflective Structured Dialogue (RSD) and trained hundreds of people all over the world. It was my involvement in the Public Conversations Project's Abortion Dialogues back in 1996 that got me started on this road. As I mentioned previously, Laura R. Chasin founded PCP in 1990. She had been witnessing on television the angry, heated debate on abortion on TV. The moderator tried in vain to engage the two sides — pro-life and pro-choice — in civil discourse, eventually giving up, saying, "There's nothing going on here but a lot of noise."

So, Laura pulled together some of her colleagues from the Family Institute of Cambridge, who watched videos of the debates and brainstormed how to make them more thoughtful, respectful, and productive.

In designing dialogues between groups with such deep divides, PCP's founders recognized that the participants would need to be assured that the goal would not be to change minds or convert opinions, but to better understand each other and what life experiences led to their positions. The result: an innovative and reliable model for opening new ways of communicating on this contentious issue. Eventually, they pulled together small community groups of pro-choice and pro-life activists, conducting eighteen sessions over the next year and a half.

By the time John Salvi walked into two Boston-area women's health clinics shooting and killing two staffers in 1994, the Public Conversations Project was there to offer up this model of conflict resolution. They trained facilitators and put together a series of dialogues of pro-choice and pro-life teams, gradually building a network of people on both sides of the issue who wanted to pursue thoughtful debate. They ultimately published *The Abortion Dialogue Handbook* to help leaders in communities across the country facilitate the process. The goal: to decrease demonizing "the other" and increase understanding between the two factions. By the time I got involved in 1996, as part of the facilitators training program, the Public Conversations Project had become a force for good in this and other highly charged public disputes.

I was trained to facilitate these conversations between pro-abortion and anti-abortion forces, to help create a place where they could coexist and perhaps even live together in peace. It was a great training ground. Since then, the organization (which became Essential Partners in 2016), with its constantly evolving process, has helped bring constructive dialogue and understanding into a wide range of contentious situations, including gun control and other politicized animosities.

From my start as a trainee, then as a volunteer, eventually as Program Director for many years, and in my most recent Senior Associate role, I have always felt it was an honor to be part of the evolution of the Public Conversations Project/Essential Partners and witness its positive impact on so many people in so many diverse situations.

Over the years we've seen the growth of the process that we eventually named Reflective Structured Dialogue. It's a formula that includes preparation — explaining the structure and asking questions of each participant before the dialogue is held — as well as active listening, civil discourse, speaking only for oneself, thinking through problems together, and much more. It never ceases to amaze me how reliable the process is at producing honest and frank community dialogues through an open evaluation of the issues at hand, and how well it leads to a deeper understanding and increased tolerance for diversity of thought, belief, and even lifestyle.

One interesting aspect of this work has been seeing what

motivates people to seek this kind of intervention. It takes a willingness to engage openly and honestly, and to really listen to the other. Some want to improve a family relationship; others want better coexistence with neighbors and community factions; still others finally decide they want to live without conflicts that may have been part of their world for years.

What always helped when we were beginning our work in a new situation was to start by giving participants questions on which to reflect. When they think about — and then share — those experiences in their lives that shaped and that now underlie their beliefs, my job as a guide became much easier. Because only then could I help them identify which things are deal-breakers and where they discover they can be flexible.

In 2019, I "semi-retired" into a Senior Associate role at EP. I continued working on projects for Essential Partners, spent more time on board work for MBBI (Mediators Beyond Borders International — more on that later), and traveled to Indonesia twice in three months to train and participate in MBBI's annual conference. And Andrea and I had a little more time for our own travel experiences. We have been to Mexico, France, Italy, Costa Rica, Greece, Turkey, Morocco, Great Britain, Spain, Amsterdam, and South Africa, as well as Armenia, Kazakhstan, and Rwanda— where our son Jesse was posted with Peace Corps and USAID, respectively—and the Bahamas, for a niece's destination wedding. Within the United States, we've been to almost every state. Our last pre-Covid trips were a self-guided civil rights tour of the South, a guided tour of Cuba with my sisters and their spouses, and a family trip to Disneyworld with our grandkids and their parents. Everywhere we traveled, we sought the unusual, off-the-beaten-track sights. We loved to meet people and to appreciate the food, art, music, botanical gardens, and street life of different cultures.

WHERE THE PROFESSIONAL AND PERSONAL MEET

I would say that in each of my relationships — with my family, friends, and colleagues — I have tried to embody what I've learned in mediation and dialogue in the ways I relate to others, with various degrees of success at various times. When confronting any conflict, I've worked at examining our backgrounds, our aspirations, and our goals.

Parenthood, especially when my own kids became adolescents, gave me a lot more empathy for the parents of all the teenagers I'd worked with over the years. When I used to consult with the police at Ayer, a couple of the guys became my friends. They'd come into my office and sit down and tell me about the kids they'd picked up high and out of their minds. I knew that they'd seen these kids at their worst, and the parents had to deal with it too. And I acknowledged the differences between my supportive role and theirs, and tell myself that I've got it easy.

We were fortunate that the issues we faced with our kids remained well within the normal range of struggles kids go through growing up. But Andrea and I recognized that when our younger son Seth was in his mid-teens, he often required more active engagement than he was convinced he needed. I was able to tap into some of the skills I'd learned on the job to help me in my own parenting: working at building bridges became an important part of my relationship with Seth then and with every relationship I've had since. I'm very grateful to have rewarding relationships with my sons and to be married to a woman who values my relationships with them and who gives me important feedback, which at many times has helped to keep me calm in stressful circumstances.

But whatever the situation, personal or professional, I began to see that resolving any problem always begins with a basic tenet of mediation: acknowledging our differences, be they gender-based, religious, generational, or political. I learned that if we're smart, in every one of our relationships we find ways to recognize what experiences, history, and values we share, and which ones we differ on, those things on which we'll naturally agree and others where we won't see things the same way at all.

I also learned - and this would be increasingly important in dealing with our own kids - that no two children grow up in the same family. What I mean is that each family member's unique personality traits cause them to interact slightly differently with every other family member. And that one of the symptoms of a relationship that doesn't work (or is no longer working) is when one or more of the people involved insists that the relationship has to stay the same, no matter how circumstances may change. The truth is that in every relationship, we need to be open to disagreement and also to reassess our assumptions, our positions, and sometimes even the roles we play with each other. We need to continually evolve in order to keep our relationships healthy.

TEACHING THESE SKILLS

What makes a great teacher? It's a question I've asked myself many times, beginning really with Upward Bound during my college years, then in Africa with the Peace Corps, in the Newton alternative school, and years later while training facilitators to do the work of dialogue.

I've come to the conclusion that being a great teacher entails having a genuine curiosity about the students in the class — what underlies their interest in learning. To really teach, we need to know who the students are — their interests and passions.

Problems arise when we teachers see ourselves as transmitters of content and believe that's our sole job. Yes, we need to be excellent transmitters, but a great teacher is also someone who is also actively engaged in learning who the students really are and connect with them in ways that give opportunities to reflect on the meaning and value to them of the particular subject.

True education nurtures students' abilities to take in new information and integrate it into their emerging understanding of the world. It's about taking the information, mixing it up and applying it to old assumptions and seeing what can be learned from this new arrangement.

Adolescents are still open to change, and we need to help them channel the energy and excitement they feel into questions that allow them to feel heard and explore new understandings of their world. That's why they are so much fun — and so challenging — to teach.

As parents, Andrea and I were looking for this kind of learning experience for our sons. When we moved from a small town in Massachusetts with mediocre public schools to Providence, Rhode Island, we expected to send them to public school. That was important to me because of my father's long service in the Buffalo public school system, and because I was concerned about elitism in private schools. But the public middle school Jesse would have attended was in turmoil, and it was not clear that it was even physically safe. Thankfully, we found the Community Preparatory School in Providence, which both boys attended. Community Prep, while private, is an independent middle school that has a core tenet of serving a culturally and economically diverse student body with a rigorous academic program in an atmosphere of mutual respect. At the time Jesse attended, that diversity included a group of great kids from the Rhode Island School for the Deaf. Not only did he have the opportunity to learn sign language as an after-school activity, but his best friend for years was one of the students from that school. In Seth's class, as the only white kid, he joked, "Can I apply for Classical (the academic magnet public high school) as a minority?"

Jesse, our elder son, took a fairly traditional approach to college at SUNY Binghamton (formerly Harpur College, my alma mater). After he graduated, he moved west, skiing, hiking, climbing, and traveling the world from his base in the Vail Valley of Colorado. After several years, during which he had pursued emergency

51

medical training mainly to deal with situations in the low-resource and remote settings he often visited, he realized it was time to get serious about some kind of career, and he joined the Peace Corps. Since he came armed with EMT training, he was assigned to work as a school health instructor in Shamb, a small village in Armenia. After the two-year stint overseas, he earned his master's in public health (MPH) at the Mailman School at Columbia University. He spent a year in Tajikistan as a Fulbright Scholar doing research on tuberculosis, worked as a global health consultant, and then joined USAID (the United States Agency for International Development) as a health officer in the Foreign Service. We have visited Jesse in so many interesting places we would likely never have experienced otherwise, including his first post in Kazakhstan and then Rwanda. These days he's easier to reach as he's posted in Washington, DC, so we get to see him and his two beautiful sons, now ages eight and four, more often.

Seth took a different, but equally fulfilling path. Feeling less than satisfied after his first year at Andrea's alma mater, the University of Wisconsin, Madison, Seth told us he didn't believe he was taking advantage of the college experience and needed a break. He ended up having a powerful transformative educational experience at the National Outdoor Leadership School, where he participated in winter camping and hiking and earned college credit for field work in the Wind River Valley in Wyoming. NOLS had a positive life-changing impact on him, giving him self-assurance and many of the skills he now uses in his work in the world of corporate healthcare.

Following college graduation, Seth managed the Rhode Island Rock Gym for a couple of years, where he met Jodie, the woman who would become his wife. They then drove and rock-climbed their way cross-country and settled in California, where he worked for an office supply firm. They came back east so he could pursue his MBA at Boston University. Following a successful ten years at two major healthcare-related corporations, Seth started Summit Health, his own consulting practice. Neither Andrea nor I understand much of what he does, but it has something to do with the intersection of healthcare and technology and multi-sided platforms and he's apparently, but not surprisingly, quite knowledgeable and excels at what he does! He and Jodie blessed us with our first grandchild in 2011, and then produced a beautiful baby boy three years later.

With four healthy grandkids and loving family relations, a happy, mutually supportive marriage and work that I love, I know how truly blessed I am.

CHAPTER 5
HEALING A WORLD CRYING OUT FOR PEACE

As I think must be evident by now, ever since my Peace Corps days I've been engaged in how my colleagues and I can adapt the lessons we've learned about the power of true dialogue and apply them to the many problems that involve people from very different cultures. Now the time had come to share what we have learned and practiced with communities across the United States and around the globe.

Looking back on the many kinds of problems we addressed on nearly every continent what impresses me is how many of Essential Partners' (EP – formerly Public Conversations Project) principles of Reflective Structured Dialogue we can adapt to people living anywhere in the world and dealing with very different challenges.

When I started traveling to different regions and working with people who were struggling with conflict, I was able to see first-hand how universal the problems of alienation are and how equally universal is the path to healing these rifts. By healing, I don't necessarily mean solving the problem, but improving relationships through reflective discussion and dialogue to the point that people were now able to co-exist, to live together in relative peace — often for the first time in years.

At EP I learned about dialogue from and worked with many brilliant practitioners, but I also became intrigued with the work of the organization Mediators Beyond Borders International (MBBI). MBBI is a volunteer-driven organization. The MBBI motto, "Building local skills for peace and promoting mediation worldwide," resonates deeply with me. It says so much about what we've been working towards for the last two decades. I joined as a volunteer, but fortunately some MMBI projects also fell within the purview of my job at EP and became joint projects. I have deeply valued my involvement as a Mediators Beyond Borders member, board member, and, for several years, its Board Chair.

The following are among my most memorable projects with both organizations.

Burundi: 2006-2008, Essential Partners: Our assignment was to help build trust after a terrible civil war. Hutu, Tutsi, and Twa villagers and townspeople, who were recovering from years of violence, viewed each other with distrust, fear, and anger. The issues of exile and newly arrived refugees, competing political loyalties, land inheritance, and class systems all constituted barriers to any sort of peace or sense of community, and blocked the road to desperately needed economic growth.

At the time, I wrote about the situation this way: "Burundi is a nation full of dignified people trying to live together across significant differences. Self-segregation, gender differences, and divisive conflicts between survivors and perpetrators of the violent civil war were all challenging aspects of Burundi's legacy."

In Burundi I was representing the Public Conversations Project which, along with the U.S.-based Conflict Management Partners and the Burundi-based Community Leadership Center, had been hired by the United States Institute of Peace to do dialogue training and conflict resolution.

Most of our work was conducted during a five-day workshop where we trained eighteen Burundian leaders who represented the different factions. They were involved in the design and facilitation of the dialogues, and afterwards, they evaluated the process. Their response was deeply gratifying. One of the leaders told us she "realized that by using this dialogue approach, people could talk of what is deep in their heart, especially things that have harmed them."

The groups then went on to design their own pilot dialogues, which they conducted in small towns and villages around the country. They taught more than one hundred residents the principles of civil discourse, and how to apply these principles to their communities' problems. We also helped the dialogue leaders put together a guide to leave behind to help them use these skills as they continued to work together to build peace.

Liberia: 2007-2011, Mediators Beyond Borders International
Also recovering from a brutal civil war, the people of Liberia were stuck in many of the same alienating patterns and festering violence in which Burundians had found themselves. Many of them had witnessed horrendous acts of violence, many were victims of gender-based violence, and many were forced to perpetrate violence on their own community members.

Ginny Morrison and Prabha Sankaranarayan of MBBI were already involved in the Liberian Initiative when I joined them in 2010. The team worked with our local partner, Society Missions of Africa (based in Accra) to create a mediation service for and by Liberian refugees who were housed in a camp in Ghana. We strengthened the mediation skills of several Ghanaian officials in partnership with Accra's Centre for Conflict Resolution. And, as the communities were preparing for the return of the refugees, we offered numerous conflict management trainings in Liberia through churches, the University of Liberia, and youth groups. We also encouraged the establishment of Youth Crime Watch of Liberia, which continues today to work in the areas of crime prevention, youth empowerment, and employment.

We also reached out to at-risk young people who had lived through frightening times, many of them as former child soldiers who had been directed to commit atrocities in their own villages. In partnership with the psychology department of the University of Ghana, Legon, we were able to support their trauma recovery work. Our team, led by National Ex-Combatants' Peacebuilding Initiatives ("NEPI"), facilitated the reintegration of seventy-five ex-fighters into communities with vocational training and hiring advocacy, as well as psychosocial support for both the former fighters and the communities that had been terrorized in the war.

Subsequently, the team partnered with peacebuilders from NEPI, RECEIVE and the Peacebuilding Resource Center. We trained them as facilitators to lead dialogues, to understand the effects of trauma, and to respond supportively to resolving conflicts without violence. The project also covered the economic level by teaching sustainable agriculture techniques, joint farming and marketing skills, as the facilitators gathered the same women for dialogues throughout the project. This eventually set the stage for peaceful co-existence and community acceptance of women of nine ethnic groups displaced there.

I found this to be one of the most effective initiatives we created in Liberia. We all hoped the women could find healing and integration, and that as mothers and wives, they would be willing to form a united front against threats of violence in these communities, and they did.

Nigeria: 2008-2015, Essential Partners: Religious violence between Muslims and Christians was running high in Nigeria: it was responsible for the killing of more than 20,000 people over the preceding ten years. The situation prompted Darren Kew of the University of Massachusetts' Center for Peace, Democracy, and Development to ask Essential Partners to lead a dialogue workshop for twenty Nigerian leaders who had come to UMass as part of a cultural exchange program.

In support of this new program, the next year EP "volunteered" my time to travel to Nigeria and meet, and begin collaborating with, two key players: Imam Mohammed Ashafa and Pastor James Wuye who together had founded the Interfaith Mediation Centre to tackle this deadly situation. My EP partner in this work was Seth Karamage, a Rwandan who went on to become a very dear friend and my "African son."

This was the first of seven trips I'd make to Nigeria over seven years. As I wrote at the time: "Extending religious tolerance and interfaith understanding are acute humanitarian needs in this country and elsewhere — and keys to political stability and development. Hope for coexistence is steadily sown through the surprising and impressive partnership of the pastor and imam, who exemplify how different religious backgrounds need not divide but rather lay a foundation of mutual respect for one another's faiths, as an antidote to terrorism, fanaticism, bigotry, and extremism."

In partnership with Pastor Wuye and Imam Ashafa and other local leaders who brought coexistence values rooted in their respective religious traditions into the process, over the next three years we created a hybrid dialogue model designed specifically for the troubles of their region. We also lent them support as they worked to bridge some pretty heated ethnic and religious divides. We led workshops bringing Christians and Muslims together in nine states across northeastern Nigeria, and we trained close to 2,000 community members in their own hybrid dialogue process. In turn, they shared the process with countless of their fellow countrymen, helping move many people to a place where those on both sides were less likely to respond to their differences in anger. And, as such, it was one of the most meaningful projects in which I have ever participated.

The words of one of the Muslim leaders, Imam Sani Isah, were rewarding: "Most important, together we are sowing a seed that will germinate and become a source of the antidote to terrorism, fanaticism, bigotry, and extremism."

All along, our goal was not only to quell the violence, but also to ease the tensions that existed beneath the surface between groups with very different identities. Here, as elsewhere around the world, our approach to dialogue has allowed trust to develop, deepening mutual understanding, and building new relationships that can serve as the foundation for a pluralist, inclusive, peaceful society. There is much work to be done in Nigeria — efforts like this one are still much needed.

Thailand: 2015, Mediators Beyond Borders International: Religious leaders in southern Thailand were seeking to develop workshops aimed at addressing the religious conflict in their country though interfaith dialogue between Christians and Muslims. Organized by Dr. Ampron Mardent, an alumna of MBBI's International Peace Training Institute and in collaboration with Walailak University, our project responded to this request. The Thais' goal was to learn new and better ways to engage in conflict prevention and transformation, and to share these approaches widely.

Prabha and I trained eighteen leaders, who in turn went on to organize dialogue groups in their own communities. In this way our original small group continued to plant the seeds for the future well-being of the people deeply affected by the decades-long violence in southern Thailand.

Indonesia: 2019 and after, Mediators Beyond Borders International We were invited by another alumna of the International Peace Training Institute, Ruby Khalifa, to support community leaders as they addressed the growing violence among Muslim groups in Indonesia. Their work focused on social cohesion and security, by building strong, peaceful Islamic communities to better resist violent extremists.

Through structured dialogues co-created with our local partner, Asia Muslim Action Network (to ensure that we had their context), these communities took on such sensitive and challenging topics such as violence within the community, child marriage, wearing of the hijab, polygamous marriage, relations with non-Muslims, women's education, and so forth. From the start, the twenty-six women who came together made enormous strides toward understanding one another. The very process of coming together for the training, and challenging themselves (and us) to take the risks of exercising genuine curiosity and authentic engagement, led to their deep commitment to expand this work in their home communities across Indonesia.

It was gratifying for all of us on the team to discover how welcoming participants were to the idea of adapting the processes and skills as dialogue facilitators. They were then able to spread the work throughout their own communities in ever-widening circles of skill-building, understanding, and peaceful coexistence.

Recently, following their extraordinary success with Reflective Structured Dialogue in 2019-2020, the leaders decided that they would expand these practices to tackle the serious challenges of reintegrating former ISIS fighters back into their communities. Twenty-five men and women from a wide range of social service, government, and civil society organizations came together, after much careful preparation, to participate in an extensive Dialogue and Restorative Practice process. The group, which is continuing this work under the name "Dangerous Dialogues and Courageous Conversations," is using these practices to thoughtfully design a first-of-its-kind program in Indonesia. They aim to integrate the fighters in the spirit of peaceful coexistence with safety and security for all.

Essential Partners Projects Closer to Home: At the same time that we and MBBI were increasingly doing peace-making work on an international stage, there were numerous situations here in the U.S. where EP was called on to help inject civil discourse into a troubled atmosphere. Among those in which I was most involved were:

City Revitalization in Flint, Michigan: 2005-2006: Flint had once been a thriving community, its prosperity centered on the automobile industry. But by the 1990s, many of those jobs had been lost to overseas factories, and unemployment and crime were on the rise. In this environment, and as neighborhoods deteriorated, racism raised its ugly head and morale was low, particularly among youth, many of whom were experiencing a sense of hopelessness.

The people at the Ruth Mott Foundation, a Flint-based charitable organization, decided something had to be done and contracted with EP to train civil society leaders to collaborate on a project designed to spearhead a planned community revitalization. Over a two-year period, we trained seventy people to facilitate dialogues about a variety of hot-button community issues, including affirmative action and school reform.

As I wrote at the time, "Seeing the connections participants made with other committed Flint leaders and how they reached out to each other to support community initiatives was a heartening shift amidst the city's many challenges."

Mental Health and the Challenges of Restraint and Seclusion: 2006-2008: A federally-funded project to reduce and ultimately eliminate the use of restraint and seclusion in all child and adolescent inpatient and intensive residential treatment facilities was being facilitated in Massachusetts by a team of mental health clinicians, administrators, and "consumer-survivors." The group had been collaborating well until one team member spoke in a way that negatively triggered others. At that point meeting together to do the work became impossible and the project was in jeopardy of failing. EP was brought in to create a process to help the various constituencies re-develop the trust needed to work cohesively again.

In an effort to heal wounds and reweave the fabric of connection and community, my colleague Bob Stains and I worked with a planning group comprised of people from each constituency and who had differing opinions about how to deal with the issues the one team member had triggered in others. Our work together, carried out over seven months, culminated in a dialogue about these emotionally charged experiences which was deeply transformative. The full team was then able to resume its work, creating policies that reduced the use of seclusion and restraint by over eighty percent.

Randolph-Macon College: Helping a Women's College Deal with Going Co-Ed: 2006-2008: In 2007, in an effort to address the financial challenges many single-sex schools experience, the board of directors of Randolph-Macon Women's College in Virginia decided to admit male students and change its name to Randolph College. But they did not expect the deep divides this would cause. There were female seniors who rejected the idea of graduating from a coed school, and the male freshmen were often made to feel unwelcome. What's more, many faculty members, trustees, and alumnae alike were upset by the decision, even though they were concerned about the financial strains.

That was the situation we found when Corky Becker, one of the founders of Essential Partners, and I arrived on campus. Charged with helping students, faculty, alumnae, and leadership recover their lost sense of community, we spent the next fifteen months bringing hundreds of faculty, staff, and students together in small groups to share their hopes, expectations, and frustrations about the change to coeducation, the impact on the college's finances, and other factors affecting campus morale. As usual, we also trained others - in this case faculty, staff, and students - to continue on as facilitators for constructive dialogues as other issues arose. That way, as they worked to continue to rebuild the trust and unity they had lost in the fray, we were able to leave a more cohesive and resilient campus community than the one we found there in 2006.

A Dialogic Campus at Bridgewater College: 2013 and Beyond: At Bridgewater College, also in Virginia, Essential Partners was selected to help create the Academic Citizenship project, an initiative to help students see themselves as important members of the campus community and not just passive receivers of an education and a degree.

The administration also knew that in order to succeed, their Academic Citizenship project would need to connect students' desire for academic success in the classroom (which most already possessed to a great extent) to the rest of their lives on campus, based on a more inclusive social life and a sense of civic pride and communal belonging.

I was on my own for this project, but the Bridgewater team was totally committed and supportive. Since by then we knew that a key method for growing these commitments and building community is to train people in Reflective Structured Dialogue, I kicked off our involvement with a workshop. The event was designed to teach faculty and staff to model these concepts, and in turn, train a core of student leaders to engage their peers in this approach.

Surprising even to me and the team, that initial workshop became the first step in a long-term collaboration that continues to train faculty and students to lead dialogues in curricular and co-curricular activities. Bridgewater's "Curriculum for College Student Life" incorporates "practicing effective communication skills in civil discourse and effective conflict resolution."

As administration and faculty began to empower students in campus leadership roles, including dialogues designed to make sure everyone feels heard and valued, the unexpected benefits of a more cohesive campus community have included better student learning outcomes and a greater sense of belonging among first-generation college students.

Welcoming Immigrant Communities in New Hampshire: 2013-2014: Welcoming America, with a branch in New Hampshire, is a nonprofit, nonpartisan organization that leads a movement in which inclusive communities become more prosperous by ensuring that everyone belongs. Over the past quarter century, the state of New Hampshire has seen an influx of immigrants and refugees from countries including those from Nepal, Vietnam, Bhutan, India, Rwanda, and Ethiopia — especially in larger cities like Manchester.

Adjustment hasn't always been easy, either for the newcomers or the long-established residents who now are now faced with accepting what their community looks like.

To navigate what was often a heated debate on immigration policy, Welcoming America partnered with local organizations and agencies that were lining up to support the new refugees. But even such like-minded groups often ended up stymied, squabbling over conflicting goals, meager resources, and divergent cultural and personal styles.

After the Essential Partners team — myself and an EP founder Maggie Herzig — were brought into the Manchester group, we trained dozens of leaders from both the immigrant and the long standing resident constituencies in RSD. By using their new skills to solve problems, they were able to overcome their history of argument and stalemate, and slowly but surely they're taking steps toward a communal vision for the Manchester of tomorrow.

As one participant told us after a breakthrough session, "We've accomplished more in the past hour than we have in the previous year."

Bay View, The Challenge to a Community's Identity: 2014-2015: This long-established Methodist summer retreat center on the shores of Lake Michigan was struggling with a controversy over inheritance of property and the future identity of the community. The bylaws specified that the ownership of a cottage can only be passed on to heirs who are members of a church with a letter from the heir's pastor. Over the years, some owners' children married out of the faith or simply did not belong to a church. Owners wanted to be able to pass on their cottages to their children, regardless of the bylaws, and children wanted to be part of the community even if not active churchgoers. This faith community was torn by lawsuits and even vandalism and verbal accusations of bigotry and godlessness. Two brave women with opposite views did some research to find help, and then approached the community with the suggestion to bring us in to help. EP's co-executive director John Sarrouf and I flew out and met with a group of leaders whom we eventually trained and who founded the initiative Bay View Listens. In turn, they went on to train others, and supported several years of dialogue. After a long, difficult process, they eventually resolved the dispute with a mutually agreeable solution.

Leadership and Civil Discourse with the Wexner Foundation: 2017: Focused on developing Jewish leaders in North America and Israel for more than thirty-five years, the Wexner Foundation has trained thousands of Wexner Fellows to step up as the next generation of Jewish leadership.

Essential Partners was brought in to help empower these alumni by giving them tools to create more effective civil discourse concerning the most pressing challenges being faced by their communities. On this project I was joined by John Sarrouf and a talented young woman from the next-gen cadre, Natalie Russ.

Unlike our other projects, this one would have feet in both the domestic and the international spheres: although Wexner is based in the US, building skills for dialoguing within Israel and with Arab leaders in the Mideast was also on the table.

This project was particularly meaningful to me as a Jew. I have spent my life working for peace, and I long for my own people to enjoy more of it.

The Foundation's hope in contracting with Essential Partners was to empower alumni to facilitate constructive dialogues about their differences. So we trained them to develop their facilitation skills through EP's dialogue process in order to bring people in their communities closer together.

The project opened with a four-day Civic Engagement training for more than sixty alumni from both the US and Israel. Over the next ten months, these alumni engaged in consultation sessions with us which were tailored to their specific community and focus. Each of the alumni came as part of a team seeking to create a bridge-building project. The twenty-odd initiatives that resulted included these: designing interfaith dialogues between Israeli Muslims and Jews; police-community dialogues in predominantly Arab cities in Israel; trans-partisan conversations inside the American Jewish community; and intergenerational dialogues in Tel Aviv.

....

Working on all of these projects, both abroad and closer to home, over the last twenty years, I was constantly reminded that, no matter how far apart two communities are — Flint, Michigan and Nigeria, for example — the roadblocks we face in our struggle to coexist in peace and mutual respect are astonishingly similar.

"All wars are civil wars, because all men are brothers."
François Fénelon

CHAPTER 6
BLESSED TO DO THE WORK I LOVE

I feel incredibly blessed that I've been able to do work that I love as an agent for advancing the cause of global peacemaking that's so near and dear to me. How many people can say they have such an opportunity, to devote a career to doing something they care so passionately about?

I've been fortunate to do this work for more than twenty years around the world, including in the United States, Canada, Greece, Nigeria, Thailand, Liberia after a civil war, and Nigeria during interreligious violence. I've also been privileged to work with talented, dedicated people who are inspired and inspiring as they build bridges to peace.

I was honored to be commissioned as a Kentucky Colonel, the highest honor bestowed by the Governor of Kentucky, for "noteworthy accomplishments and outstanding service to our community, state, and nation."

And in November 2021, the Center for Mediation and Collaboration of Rhode Island will recognize me as the first recipient of their Peace Maker Award* at the 25th anniversary of this organization. This award is especially meaningful as I was a founder and Executive Director of this local organization, and had rejoined the board in 2020. (* *This award was presented posthumously on November 4, 2021.*)

It's also been gratifying that, over the years, MBBI's peacebuilding work has been recognized by two prestigious awards. We were the 2016 recipient of Association of Conflict Resolution's Outstanding Leadership Award, which honors exceptional work promoting conflict resolution in local communities around the globe, particularly in challenging or demanding circumstances.

We received the other of these honors, the Cardozo Journal of Conflict Resolution's International Advocate for Peace Award in 2020, specifically for the work we did in partnership with local leaders in Liberia. In receiving this award, we were honored to join a distinguished group of previous recipients including

President Bill Clinton, Beatle Paul McCartney and Archbishop Desmond Tutu, among others.

In my acceptance speech that night I said these words that, looking back over the years, truly reflect the beliefs that continue to motivate everything I do, a philosophy that also represents those ideals for which MBBI has always stood.

"I'd like to share with you some of the values and principles that guided that work (in Liberia) and that continue to underlie our approach as we strive to build local capacity for peace and to fulfill our vision of creating a more peaceable world.

In many of the contexts in which we've worked, we're "outsiders," so it's essential for us to view the work in terms of collaboration and partnership, because it's always the local people who must be at the center of these kinds of efforts. Because we know from experience that it's the people themselves who build the peace, not outsiders. As we share our mediation, dialogue, reconciliation, and other practices in response to local requests, it's always with a deep awareness of the importance of adapting them to the local context and culture. We view our role as elevating, amplifying, and supporting the voices of local people. 'Voice' is a core value for us. Our role as mediators and peacebuilders is to help create the spaces in which local voices can be heard, by each other and by those in power.

Peace is not just the absence of conflict. Rather it's a positive commitment to the values of voice, connection, and community.

When it comes to voice, in every project I've been a part of I've seen that one of the most basic human needs is to be heard. The power of narrative, of people telling their stories, expressing their needs and being deeply heard, lies at the heart of conflict transformation, connection, and building (or repairing) community. We also value ubuntu, the South African term that speaks of social connection and relationship. "I am because we are," speaks to the sense that we are all connected, all human beings, and that our differences don't inherently need to lead to conflict. The poet Audre Lorde said that 'it's not so much our differences that divide us, but rather how we deal with those differences.'

Imam Muhammed Sani Isah of Nigeria's Interfaith Mediation Center said that our approach is "about using words to deal with our differences, rather than machetes." The challenge so often is for people to learn how to live together or how to live together again. And what we know is that connection and relationship make it possible and likelier for people to co-exist, acknowledging their similarities, as well as their differences.

Sangha, the Sanskrit word for "community," also connotes the value that is at the heart of our approach. Supporting and enhancing local communities and their resilience are critical as it's at the community level that healing takes place most effectively for societies dealing with trauma. Our work in Liberia (and all over the world) is characterized by creating and strengthening community. It's harnessing the power of sangha to address the healing that's needed in our work, whether it's in Liberia, in Indonesia, in Nigeria, or in the United States.

Our approach to building local capacity for peace is also distinguished by its focus on re-humanization of the "other." We create spaces within which people can again experience each other as neighbors, as community members with aspects of shared identity, as well as differences, and as three-dimensional human beings, not simply as the stereotypes we are prone to experiencing the "other" as in times of conflict and polarization.

In the words of one of our Liberian partners at the conclusion of a workshop that we did there, "As a former rebel, I think that perhaps if we had known about this approach, we would not have had a civil war."

Gratifications and High Points

As gratifying as it's been to witness how the benefits of dialogue and civil discourse have found recognition in the larger world, the real rewards of my work are more intimate: when someone in a workshop or dialogue thanks us for asking a question that opens a door for them to be heard, or when someone else tells me, "I carry the lessons I've learned with me into my work every day."

Can you see things from two perspectives simultaneously and empower others to do so too? In my case, coming in with those two foundations — teaching and therapy — under my belt was crucial to my being able to develop, refine, and integrate foundational peacemaking skills and transmit them to people around the world so they can go ahead with the process of building real peace.

Indonesia, 2019 MBBI International Congress:
with Nobel Peace Prize winner Jose Ramos-Horta

Liberia, 2010-2011:
conflict management training to
create sustained peace post-civil war

Indonesia 2019: conducting an MBBI workshop

Liberia circa 2010: L-R me, Winny, Ginny Morrison, unknown, and Bill Sa

Cambridge, Laura's Retirement from PCP, May 22, 2006:
Back row L-R: John Case, Board member, Johanna Chao Rittenburg,
Board Member, Mary Jane McGlennon, Board Chair, Sallyann Roth,
Founding Associate, me (David Joseph, Associate), Howard Garsh,
Board Treasurer, Manda Adams, Training Coordinator, and Maggie Herzig,
Founding Associate.

Middle row: L-R: Bob Stains, Associate, Susan Wheeler, Director of Administration, Dick Chasin, Founding Associate, Laura Chasin, Founder and Director, Bill Madsen, Associate, Talya Bosch, Associate Director, and Meenakshi Chakraverti, Associate.

Front Row: L-R :Mahvash Hassan, Marketing Coordinator, Susan Dowd, Grant Writer, Christie Wren, Executive Assistant, Corky Becker, Founding Associate, and Bill Kaplan, Operations and IT Manager.

Indonesia 2019:
Being a Proud Disruptor
(L)Prabha Sankarnaranayan, President of MBBI and
Raihal Fajri, Alum of MBBI's Global Peace Building Training
Institute and (R) Executive Director Katahari Institute, Indonesia

Pittsburg, PA at Diwali Celebration, 2018: Mini MBBI reunion
Back row L-R Andrea, me, Jim Longo, Mary Jo Harwood,
Pat Montague.
Seated L-R Ginny Morrison, Sankar Sankarnaranayan,
Prabha Sankarnaranayan, Mary Montague.

Smithfield, RI circa 2014:
with son Seth Joseph and my African son Seth Karamage

A Quarter Century of Empowering Peace

I was fortunate to be one of the right people in the right place at the right time to be able to help move this dialogue and constructive conversation approach forward. In my case, as I've mentioned, I do think it helped that I came to the field with a background as both a psychotherapist and, like my father before me, a teacher. So many of the principles of Reflexive Dialogue have their roots in family therapy and education. With disadvantaged kids for Upward Bound while I was still in college, then with African teens for the Peace Corps, and later in an alternative high school in Massachusetts — those experiences made the dialogue training feel like a natural extension of teaching. They gave me what I needed to build on, to teach my students what they needed to know.

This rule of successful teaching is the identical process when we're working toward peacemaking: to learn the participants' values, their strengths, and their needs so you can understand what will appeal to them and what will leave them cold. And to appreciate in what way they will be able to truly see the humanity of each other as individuals, and their similarities, that we are created by the same God, and eventually begin to understand why "they" don't believe exactly what "I" believe.

Beginning in the 1980s and '90s, a lot of people were tired of all the anger and bickering that weren't getting anyone anywhere constructive. They were tired of the idea that if you don't win you're a loser, and they saw how easy it is close your mind to the other point of view and jump to judge by using a lot of unflattering stereotypes. Many had begun to recognize the high cost of conflict — whether in families, on a community level, nationally or internationally. One sign of this awareness: the phrase "win-win" began to appear in public.

What we began to see back then was that when conflicts occur and the only thing on the table is the area of disagreement, the issues might get hashed out, but the relationships almost always deteriorate. We could only see the guy on the other side pointing at us, saying "We've got a problem and the problem is you."

For dialogue to work, we have to begin to look at what values and experiences we have in common, and understand where they came from, in order to be able to see our differences through the lens of our opponents. When we begin to see our common values and mutual interests, as well as our different needs and different goals, only then can a relationship begin to grow. Then peaceful co-existence becomes possible.

Eventually, if it's done right with partners who are open to it, you can achieve a growth in trust that makes for a greater degree of resiliency in the face of disagreement. Establishing that trust has been the goal of every project I've worked on, so when we leave, the tools for dialogue remain behind with the communities as a buffer to keep future disagreements from turning ugly.

In Liberia after the civil war, those who had fought were heavily stigmatized. No one was in any hurry to welcome them back into the community because they had committed some horrific atrocities against their own villages, even their own families. The National Ex-Combatants Peacebuilding Initiative was a remarkable organization composed of men and women who had fought, but had come to recognize the harm they had done and wanted to atone for that. They actively set out to try to rebuild community, and by their actions to exhibit a different kind of leadership.

Many of the issues in Liberia were some of the same issues that came up here in the United States in connection with immigration issues. I'm referring to fascinating questions such as "who are we," "who is our community," and "who gets to define that?" I think that community is a powerful source — at least potentially — of support and nurturance and guidance for us. But if the community is built only on stereotypes, it can also be a source of exclusion and poor treatment of those we deem not to be part of our community, as our own country's increasing political divide so sadly demonstrates. There's frankly no faster way of pulling a community apart, than by "othering" the opposition, a problem I continue to wrestle with.

So, when I've helped people to see similarities and areas of mutual concern, whatever the conflict, it enabled them to build the bridge they need to cross over to be able to accept their differences. That's been my experience.

And What Makes a Great Therapist?

I've also discovered that my two decades working as a psychotherapist greatly aided me in my subsequent two decades training people across the globe to engage in dialogue in an effort to build peace where rancor had been the norm. In psychotherapy, you need to be able to step outside your own theories and assumptions, and see things through the eyes of the individual, or even more so, the points of view of the husband and wife, or the teen and her parents, sitting in front of you — the whole family.

The basis of PCP's dialogue design had roots in Family Systems Theory (FST). FST is a form of psychotherapy that aims to help people resolve their problems within the context of their family, where many issues are likely to have begun. Family members work together to better understand their groups dynamics, and how the ways their individual actions affect one another and the family as a whole. One of the most important premises of Family Systems Therapy is that what happens to one member of a family happens to all family members. PCP's dialogue work began when four FST therapists at the Family Institute of Cambridge and a social scientist colleague came together to explore how their work with conflict in families might be applicable to conflicts with people in heated disagreement on issues in the public domain. A critical piece of what FST brings to dialogue is recognizing that we cannot change what another person believes, but we can change the way we react to their beliefs. It's asking — what I can do to change myself — the way I view others and interact with them — to impact others' behavior? How can I be more effective in working with other people?

The core idea is: if I try to do something differently, then maybe they will do something differently also. And I'm the best part of this system to begin the change. So it was natural that those of us with this kind of background in couples and family therapy would be among the founders of the dialogue movement. We brought many of those FST ideas to show people how to focus on changing themselves to change the situation, instead of focusing on changing other people.

Focusing on relationship makes a huge difference here. When PCP brought people together to discuss abortion, for instance, the goal was not to change how others thought, but always to understand what in their lives had led them to think and feel the way they do.

Training Community Leaders: Teaching the Skills

Where does the power to make lasting change really come from? It's only possible when you manage to empower the stakeholders. If there was one thing I learned in the years I taught teenagers, it was that the key to engaging them is to help them see what the subject at hand can mean to them. And the same thing applies when training adults in dialogue.

Teaching teens sharpened my focus and ability to be able to understand the value of the different answers that different people will give to the same question. And that knowing what's important to them — and how a more peaceful relationship will benefit them — is the first step to creating something better out of even the most difficult relationship. Ultimately it results in a better outcome with reduced aggravation and tension.

The next step - and it's a big one - is to begin to see the conflict through the other person's eyes. When we are incapable of doing that, it's because we're still wearing our own headsets.

The only way to get past that? We need to bring a genuine and non-judgmental curiosity (not about what's wrong with their thinking — why aren't they as enlightened as we are and see the world as we do? Can't they see that we are so obviously right and they just don't get it?), but how are they experiencing this situation? To do that, we need first and foremost to allow for the fact that they are seeing things differently from us because they're coming from a life experience that's different from our own, which leads them to different conclusions about the world around them.

Taking this leap is at the basis of how we as individuals, families, communities, and nations can together create a more peaceable world. It's that simple and that difficult. But, as I say, it's not impossible. I've been there when it works, and it's beautiful.

Teens are naturally open to new experiences, new ideas, and new understandings. That's why I loved working with them as a teacher and then as a therapist. But how can we help an adult open up? Adults come into a given situation with life experience and they all too often get trapped into thinking they have a lock on understanding how and why this is the way things are.

I have seen that if we create a space through Reflective Structured Dialogue, we can help adults stretch themselves to become genuinely curious about the beliefs of others, to see other views as different, instead of wrong. That ability is at the heart of what keeps life interesting, when we can take and learn what we have used (but not encase it in steel and concrete) in productive ways. That's how we can push past the conflict and begin to make real peace.

Grateful for Many Opportunities

It's been amazing to be able to learn from so many different people on four continents - Asia, Africa, North America, and Europe. I've gained so much awareness from the time I've spent working with all those families, organizations, communities, and faith groups. These people, struggling in the grip of so many different kinds of conflict, have all offered lessons to me about how much we share on the deepest level: that no matter how different we are on the outside, we are surprisingly similar within. Whether we are of different religions or races or speaking different languages, we all love our families and want the best for our children, we're all invested in our communities; all we have to do is make the shift in our own hearts that allows us to really see and hear the humanity in the other.

I am also grateful for the opportunity I had at Temple Beth El in Providence, Rhode Island where I was Board Chair for several years, and where one of my most enjoyable activities was teaching the kids at Junior Congregation on Shabbat mornings. Also gratifying were the projects we took on through the social justice committee which I chaired for several years.

Looking back, whether it was for a professional project, in my own family relationships, with friends and colleagues, my volunteer work through Mediators Without Borders, or at my temple, the basics remain the same.

The magic happens when, once others know we hear and respect them, the more likely they are to return the respect. But all too often, when they don't feel heard and understood, the reverse holds true; they will be much less likely to be willing to try to understand us. We all play an important role to make this magic come true in our lifetime - it's not okay to wait for someone else to do it. We each need to contribute what we can in order to build a better, more peaceful world.

CHAPTER 7
PEACE:
WHAT THIS WORLD NEEDS NOW
AND HOW DIALOGUE CAN HELP HERE AT HOME

Frankly, the atmosphere in our country in the last couple of years has been frightening. We've taken a giant step backwards in terms of civil discourse. Increasingly, we seem to believe that those with different opinions from us are our enemies rather than just our political opponents. Treating people with whom we disagree as enemies: I never thought I'd see this happen here in America.

I'm a political junkie. I regularly hear people supposedly listening, but really just preparing to speak, rather than listening to understand the other person or to learn something. Sadly, our media really doesn't promote understanding of the other. On the news every night I see the evidence in the disparaging, mean-spirited ways people refer to those who disagree with them on climate change, on the vaccine and masking, on gender issues, on racial equality, and more. All these issues have become heavily politicized. I find myself groaning over what the evening news chooses to report on and, just as bad, for what it chooses not to cover: constructive efforts going on everywhere to build peaceful communities.

There's a wonderful tension we have in this country between being individuals, and being individuals who together comprise a community. But now it appears we are valuing individualism over community in ways that leave many people feeling unheard and victimized. With this focus on individualism, we fail to see how our actions might have effects we don't fully intend. This individualism creates a cycle of conflict, polarization, and division that I think is dangerous for our country. We must find ways to talk together to find a richer, more complex understanding of who we and others are as individuals and as communities.

We must choose to talk together, so that each of us can have the experience of being heard by those we disagree with; so that we can express what is really important to us and be willing and courageous enough to also listen to the other side with an open mind and heart.

One of the biggest challenges in this country today is that we are increasingly choosing to segregate ourselves. More and more people choose to live among those who see the world as they do. This geographic isolation insulates us from those who think differently, and the politicization of the media — particularly TV — reinforces our divides. It's a big change from the journalism of Edward R. Murrow, Walter Cronkite, David Brinkley, and the other journalists I grew up with, and the diverse community in which I lived.

Much of the conflict today takes place on the internet, where lots of smart people get paid a lot of money to create a divisive, even-more-negative climate that only serves to separate us. And we tend to gravitate to sites representing what we already believe, and negate the others points of view. It saddens me that our children and grandchildren are growing up in this environment.

As Daniel Patrick Moynihan famously said, "Everyone is entitled to his own opinion but not his own facts." So how can we possibly arrive at a commonly recognized set of facts when the currently polarized media tell us different sets of facts are true? One of the most troubling things to me today is that some of the more distressing social factors that characterize Eastern Europe are now present here as well: there is an assault on truth, on objective facts. We have to be more active watchers and readers and do a better job of knowing the source of the facts we accept as true, and we have to ask, "Can I trust this source to tell the whole truth?" And "Where can I find evidence to support the facts I hear?"

I've been thinking about that now, because many of the recent projects I've done in our country involve people caught up in this growing divisiveness.

A great deal of research supports the idea that the easiest way to form "us" is to define "the other" so all of us can stand in opposition to them. But we've seen that this "othering," while it may feel good in the moment, doesn't address the high cost to our society, a cost that's becoming increasingly clear.

We can turn this around together only when we are challenged to be our better selves, to be the kind of people who want to help to heal a broken country, a country that has for so long been a beacon of hope and has such great potential — if only we choose to repair the damage that's been done.

What Can Each of us do to Reverse this Destructive Trend?

Whenever I am asked this question, though it may seem simplistic or too hard to do, the first thing I recommend is to seek out someone who disagrees with you. Do this for the express purpose of really listening to them, not just waiting until you can launch into defending your point of view but hearing them out and then asking questions from a position of genuine curiosity. Ultimately, there is a big difference between listening with the purpose of understanding, and listening with the purpose of responding, of debating, or being right — a kind of listening that occurs a lot these days.

It's helpful to read and watch presentations of other perspectives, but it's much more meaningful to hear the opposing view face-to-face. We can't skip this step of open-minded listening if there is to be any hope for making peace in this century. If we dismiss another's point of view because they don't share our background or worldview or if they vote for another party and see things differently, then we're doing our real enemies' work for them. As human beings sharing this globe at this moment in time, who are our real enemies? Hate, prejudice, and apathy — the dismissal of others who think differently, and detachment from the suffering of others.

I try to practice keeping an open mind myself. As the political situation has shifted in the United States, I've found myself more open to consider a more conservative point of view. I've given myself a certain freedom to rethink things and reach different conclusions than I did during my teenage years when I was more liberal. During the 1960s, '70s, and '80s my political perspective was pretty uncomplicated. As an older adult who's read and seen more of history, I have become more willing to recognize the complexity and the multiple perspectives surrounding issues. I've learned to appreciate nuances, and not to fear change. Sometimes that has led me into uncharted waters and, occasionally, to a more conservative viewpoint.

I believe that my foundational work in teaching, therapy, mediation, and dialogue has given me the courage to explore unchartered territory and that in many ways, at the end of my career I'm able to live even more authentically what I've taught and to be open to other understandings.

What Dialogue Has to Offer Today's World

Reflective Structured Dialogue offers the opportunity to be listened to and be really heard by someone who is as genuinely interested in learning about your experience as you are about theirs. Dialogue allows us to talk about the kind of world in which we want our children and grandchildren to grow up. If we can have an RSD kind of dialogue, we'll end up walking out of the room with a deeper understanding of what matters to one another, and we'll be more likely to recognize our commonalities.

Most of the time we are not even conscious of what kinds of assumptions we're making. So we need to really learn about each other instead of making assumptions based on stereotypes, such as "You're a guy, therefore..." or a "You're a woman, therefore..." or "He's someone with a particular profession, faith, race, or family status, therefore..."

I think of truth like a giant jigsaw puzzle with no agreed-upon picture to orient ourselves. It seems that, today, too many groups say, "I've got my pieces, I know what the picture looks like. I'm right and you're wrong and we need to be acting based on what I see and say." Instead, we need to hold out the possibility that there may be some value in seeing and accepting the place in the puzzle where the other group's pieces fit. When we share our pieces, we have a much better chance of understanding, and solving, what the big picture looks like, and of creating a harmonious experience of learning.

We grow up in different countries and in different families and genders and in communities with different ethnicities, religions, and experiences. We need to realize that we have an amazing wealth to share with each other if only we can slow down and engage with each other with curiosity. If we are able to move from certainty to uncertainty, and from "fear of" to "openness to" the other, then we are on a path to great benefit. But only if we can do that. I fear that if we don't do a better job of engaging with one another, our divides may damage America beyond repair.

I've come to see the mediator's job, now and in the future, as one of helping to create a way of relating to each other in a society where we are free to express our opinion - whether we agree or disagree with the prevailing beliefs — without fear of reprisal or attack. Mediators can be guides, whether working within a family or a community or a larger society. They can help all parties stop dehumanizing or stereotyping each other. The mediator can also present choices of how we can treat each other and interact, and remind us of our common humanity and goals in life.

The RSD dialogue approach helps us ask, "What do I really know about that person?" or "Why do I believe that?" And "What stereotypes might they be entertaining about me?" It starts with the willingness to look at yourself and have the courage to be able to speak what's true for you and listen with enough resilience to really hear what might be true for someone else. Listening with resilience goes back to the intention to really understand. So, when I hear something that makes me want to say, "No, you're wrong about that," I need to hold that for a minute and instead to approach difference with curiosity. What are the factors in your life experience that have shaped your beliefs that are so different from mine? We need to refrain from judging others, suspend judgments temporarily, ask questions, and listen to the answers with an open mind.

In times of polarization, when the zealots are empowered and the voices that get heard are the voices that are more extreme, screaming at each other and talking over each other, that kind of 'dialogue' is difficult; it is hardly logical. Television rarely allows us to hear from people whose views are nuanced and thoughtful. TV hosts rarely invite them to speak because they're not as entertaining as people who are yelling at each other and calling each other names. Conflict entrepreneurs take advantage of this. It sells.

But When we Invite it in, Dialogue can be the Pressure Release Valve.

Each of us needs to take responsibility for how we can engage together as citizens to build our communities, rather than tear them apart. Dialogue can make space for people whose ideals are deeply felt and expressed in ways that don't dehumanize or demonize others. I believe that this describes most Americans, even given the powerful forces that encourage us to demonize and stereotype.

Dialogue Is Needed Now

From where I sit in our living room in North Providence, Rhode Island, having worked for a half century to repair rifts and make peace around the world, and to find ways to encourage peace to emerge from enmity, where do I see dialogue skills most desperately needed now and in the foreseeable future?

Literally everywhere in public discourse, from the media to universities to families and friendships that are falling by the wayside of intolerance.

Those courageous enough to approach dialogue for the first time think they will learn something about people who have different beliefs, and they will. But after training sessions, I've often had participants approach me and say, "I had no idea I was going to reflect as deeply as I have on my own beliefs, how it comes to be that this issue is so important to me." Too often, people just adopt slogans and try to simplify why X is right and Y is wrong. So it's wonderful to hear people say that dialogue made them reflect more deeply on their own beliefs.

When I got to Nigeria to begin three years of work with our partners at the Interfaith Mediation Center, where a number of inspiring and courageous Christians and Muslims were working to build coexistence and community, the very first thing I had them do was a dialogic introduction.

Even though most of them had known one another for years, I asked them to do an introduction by talking about the spiritual teachings that inspired them to devote their lives to peacebuilding. And I asked them to tell a story about someone from their faith tradition who had inspired them. In the end, after they had shared stories, several said, "I can't believe we've worked together for twenty years but I never knew you felt that way, that that's what brought you to this work." So, a large part of what we hope for with dialogue is to invite people to talk about their passions, what inspired them, and why they feel drawn to a particular world view — enabling a conversation that brings fresh new information to the surface and reconnects participants in a different way.

A Little Advice

I'm often asked for advice by those who are determined to help promote understanding across the chasms. Some of them work in schools and on college campuses to build tolerance for multiple perspectives. Others are involved in helping families develop better relationships between spouses and kids. Still others work in organizations that help communities facing soaring crime rates, or countries torn by interfaith or interracial animosities.

Whatever the focus and whatever the playing field, what we've found is that dialogue skills, which are surprisingly easy to master, can be utilized by practitioners in any number of different fields and jobs. There are so many possible applications: a school administrator coping with angry parents pushing to ban books and even change the curriculum, a mayor of a town with hate graffiti spray-painted on its public spaces, or a minister whose congregants are fighting among themselves over political issues.

In any of these situations, and so many more, dialogue skills can help defuse tension as well as allow space for people to be heard and feel respected, and this can lead to real change.

Based on what I've witnessed and experienced, what I would say to the citizens of the world is that our countries, our people, our society will be better off when we have the benefit of hearing one another's voices. I am reminded of a wonderful line from the Koran I was taught by a Nigerian friend: "Surely if God had wanted to create us all the same, He could have done so. But He chose not to."

Research in the United States supports the idea that the way conservatives' and liberals' brains actually process information is different - it's not just our values, but the way we think. What if we bring ourselves into relationships with others around our differences and explore those differences just as we would with our children and our grandchildren?

One of the greatest lessons I've learned in working with people in so many different cultures is that, although we Americans like to think we're a very advanced society, we're now witnessing some of these same destructive patterns that less-developed countries regularly face. I would not have thought we'd need to take some of our own medicine to address issues in the US. But we do, and we've never needed it as much as we do today … and probably into the future as well.

I would encourage groups of people interested in promoting peace to connect with other similar groups. For example, faith and community groups could connect with professional associations, and governmental bodies could foster connections with the religious entities and nonprofits that serve their constituents. We must try to identify the people who are already practicing these skills, regardless of where and for what purpose. They may not know there's another group of people in another part of town who would also be interested in learning and applying these techniques in their community. One thing we've lost in living such separate lives today is that we often don't know what even our own neighbors are doing to make a difference.

Reaching across the divides, we can find a basis for trust and communication, and discover that we may have more similarities than we ever realized. We can focus our conversations on the value of kindness, how we need to be judged by our actions and not just by what we say.

We can also identify those within every group — even the "opposition" — who are genuinely open to hearing the other, capable of building mutual respect and understanding, and willing to work together to build bridges for the good of everyone involved.

Realistically, I know this message is not going to be appreciated by everyone. But there will be members of nearly every group, political party, religion, or cause for whom it will resonate.

Wouldn't it be wonderful if people who are interested in politics but who fundamentally disagree could work together to identify a list of shared values? If people within corporations — leadership and workers alike — could work to create a culture of mutual values, starting with the value of the basic golden rule: treating each other the way they want to be treated? What if we all resolve to create the kind of society that's built on the values of justice and mercy and cooperation? That vision has kept me going all these years, as I've worked in so many conflict-ridden situations around the world.

For most of us, learning to develop these skills works best when we start with the basic unit of the family. That means regularly spending the time to really listen to each other with an open mind. One tradition that developed in our family was this: our son Seth and I would have long talks about his work in the corporate sector, and chew over how he could use the "soft skills" of therapy, mediation, and dialogue to his company's advantage. As a father whose life has been about teaching others to know how to make peace in their own lives, families, and communities, it has given me enormous satisfaction to know how much value Seth places on our conversations. Andrea and I got a kick out of the fact that he came to refer to these talks as the DJI–the Dave Joseph Institute. Aware that my time is limited, I have encouraged him to carry on the tradition in his own family as it becomes the SJI– the Seth Joseph Institute.

I've found that being a father has been in large part about teaching my sons the skills to look honestly at what's working and what isn't, apply what they feel has been valuable, and pass those things along to the next generation. I am so gratified that they do all that and more.

What Makes Me Proud About — and Grateful for — This Work

When I think back on what's made me the happiest in the work I've done, what has given me the deepest satisfaction, it's been the opportunity to help train the next generation of practitioners to use dialogue techniques. Through my work at Essential Partners and Mediators Beyond Borders International, I was able to see the growth of a cadre of young people motivated to carry on the work of building understanding to calm the waters of conflict. It has been enormously gratifying to train and work with people from the younger generation, and to know that when I'm no longer able to carry on, there will be dedicated, skilled people who are continuing with this vital work.

Thinking back, I realize this opening the minds and hearts of young people has been a primary motivation for me since college, when I worked with my first Upward Bound kid from Binghamton's inner city.

I also look back with gratitude to those who came before me. We learn so much from the people who first taught us our values. This starts with our family — in my case, my father, who was so passionate about the power of education, my mother, who was deeply dedicated to social justice, and my grandparents, who lived and passed on their devotion to Jewish tradition.

My gratitude also extends to those not related by blood, but who were teachers and mentors, conveying other essential values to our young and impressionable selves. Gratitude also goes to those colleagues I have worked with for so many years with whom I share core values and a mission, whose drive for building peace has inspired me always to reach higher and do more, living and teaching the values we are all honored to pass along.

This field of making light from the darkness, understanding from alienation, peace from anger, it's been my *bashert* — Yiddish for destiny. I am realistic enough to know it can't be completed in my generation, but, in the words of the sage Rabbi Tarfon two thousand years ago: "You are not obliged to complete the work, but neither are you free to desist from it."

As I look toward the future — starting with our own children and our four grandchildren — I pray there will come a time when all the world's inhabitants learn to live together in peace.

FINDING A NEW TONE
FOR THE DAY OF ATONEMENT BY DAVE JOSEPH
(First appeared in onbeing.org in October 2005)

The Jewish new year (*Rosh Hashanah*) began last week and with it, the Days of Awe, ending with the Day of Atonement (*Yom Kippur*). During these ten days, Jews are urged to reflect on their life, to examine their actions of the past year, and to repent. It is said that this is the time when God decides whom to inscribe in the Book of Life, who will live and who will die, who will have a good life and who will not for the coming year.

The Book of Life is written on *Rosh Hashanah*, but our introspection and actions during the Days of Awe can alter God's decree before it is finalized on *Yom Kippur*. Through prayer, good deeds and *teshuvah* — which is usually translated as repentance or turning away from sin toward God — our fate can be changed. As a child, I often felt like "turning away" from *Yom Kippur,* a holiday I experienced as aversive and dread-full. The most off-putting factor wasn't so much the 24-hour fast, or even the scratchy woolen suit I had to wear to services. Rather, what was so oppressive to me was what felt like an interminable day of reflection, one that invited me to wallow in feeling ashamed of my imperfections and inadequacies.

There is one prayer in which each individual beats his or her breast while confessing to an alphabet soup of sinful actions during the past year. I dreaded *Yom Kippur* because I understood it to be an opportunity to focus primarily, if not solely, on my shortcomings. Over time I have developed a different understanding, prompted in part by an experience I had in Liberia, while teaching about dialogue. A workshop participant commented that what he really appreciated about our approach was that it encouraged "confession." Taken aback and puzzled by how dialogue could involve confession, I inquired about the meaning of his comment. He responded: "Dialogue encourages me to look deep into my heart, to have the courage to speak about what is most meaningful and important to me."

When I heard this lovely explanation, it began to make a lot more sense. In teaching about dialogue, we often talk about the opportunity to learn and better understand what is important to others; equally valuable is the opportunity to reflect deeply on our own experience, values, and beliefs. So, for my Liberian friend, "confession" meant the opportunity to slow down, to examine and give voice to what was deep in his heart.

This understanding brings me a different and much deeper appreciation of the value of *Yom Kippur*. I see it as an opportunity to slow down and to reflect, to have the courage to review my actions of the past year and to think about what kind of person I want to be in the coming year. I have also found a gentler approach to the concept of "sin" within the Jewish tradition. What I saw as only an opportunity for self-castigation, I now recognize as a time to reflect on where I have fallen short of the commitments to how I want to conduct my life. Rather than a rehearsal of my innate failings, Yom Kippur becomes an opportunity for course correction, for acknowledging where and when I have not lived out my commitments and to rededicate myself to doing better the next year.

I have also deepened my appreciation for the distinction between sins against God and sins against another person. When one has broken a commandment against God, it suffices to acknowledge the wrong, repent, and commit to not repeating the sin. When one has sinned against another person, however, reconciliation is called for, and it is incumbent upon to the individual to approach the other person, acknowledge what was done, and request forgiveness.

If the other person is not willing to forgive us, we are taught that we must ask again and even a third time, if necessary. If we have spoken from the heart and been refused three times, the sin is counted as forgiven. This primary focus on repairing the relationship, even though it may entail a difficult conversation, resonates with me. To only acknowledge in my mind what I have done, without attempting to heal the relationship and directly address my behavior with the other person, would feel inadequate.

So I'm pleased to have found a way to transform my understanding of Yom Kippur into an opportunity for "confession," reflection, healing, and turning back to the ideals that I have chosen to guide my life, even though it means that I may have some difficult conversations ahead of me.

DAVE JOSEPH'S TOOLBOX:
TEN STEPS FOR TURNING RANCOR
INTO RELATIONSHIP
AND DIVISIVENESS INTO PEACE

1. Adopt a personal willingness to self-examine. Only by acknowledging your own preconceived notions for what they are can you begin to understand others.

2. Remember that prejudice comes from the word pre-judge. Creating peace relies on viewing each person you meet as unique and deeply human.

3. Honor others' experiences. Try to imagine what they were like to live through.

4. Be curious. Say to yourself: "I wonder what it's like to be this person, and how and why that leads to those conclusions." Ask the kind of questions that will help you understand.

5. Begin with a list of those values and goals you have in common before mentioning your differences. At the end of the day, you may be surprised to discover those things you share outweigh - and may soften — those that divide you.

6. Practice forgiveness. Learn to forgive yourself and others so you can move into the future with a clean slate. Remember we are all "under construction."

7. Take a risk. Be open to changing your thinking and opinions to see things through a different lens.

8. Work together to see the big picture. Managing conflict is like putting together a jigsaw puzzle. You have your pieces, I have my pieces, and when we share our pieces we have a much better chance of understanding what the big picture looks like.

9. Remember that peace is not simply the absence of conflict. Even if things are peaceful now, conflict over some issue will likely arise at some point. Instead, see peace as a positive ongoing commitment to the values of giving voice, forging connection, and building community.

10. Ask "What can I do to bring peace to this world?" If you're concerned about the costs of conflict — to families and communities, nationally and internationally — where might you jump in to help build peace? Can you reach out to others who also yearn for a better world and support financially or as a volunteer local, national, or international organizations committed to peaceful solutions?

MESSAGES AND MEMORIES
FROM FAMILY AND FRIENDS

It's been said that a blessed life is filled with friends who are like family and family who are like friends. David's life (and mine) have been blessed in this way   Andrea Joseph

Ruth Ma'ayan Fate, Sister: My big brother David has been invaluable in helping me figure out how to manage relationships. I know I'm currently in a wonderful relationship largely because of what I've learned from him; he taught me that everyone has their own view of things and to appreciate how other people see things. To be open to other viewpoints has been huge and has really enriched my life more than I can express. Dave has this effect on everyone around him.

Bruce Connuck, Cousin: Like many of his colleagues and friends, I shared with David "upfront and personal" exposure to how ethnic and political divides can tear societies apart, sometimes with extreme violence. I saw how group mythologies, deep-seated prejudices, and deliberate misinformation or malice, often coupled with isolation from others' experiences and viewpoints, can have toxic, even lethal, consequences.

During some of the most difficult moments I encountered, one of my most called-upon defense mechanisms was to remind myself of David and the work he and his colleagues were doing to persistently chip away at some of the walls of mutual incomprehension and separation. Individuals or small groups, one by one, on and on. Not always successfully, but enough so as to validate a conviction that it can be possible for people of different groups and viewpoints, people who in some cases have had recent traumatic individual or group experiences, to sit with their opponents and at least talk.

I've known David my entire life. His passion and commitment, his readiness, even eagerness, to throw himself personally into the hard work of trying to bring people back together, back to recognition of the so simple yet so complex fact that we are all of the same group — humans — has served as an example for me. He had the best kind of idealism: the realism to know that people talking and listening to each other may not lead to agreement, coupled with the passionate conviction that we can never stop trying.

Marc Jacobs, Friend: To most people in the world, the evening of August 8, 1974 was quite historic. Richard Nixon went on television to announce his resignation as President of the United States.

For David and me, and then for the Joseph and Jacobs families, the special significance of that date is that was when David and I first met; it launched what became a year or two later a deep and everlasting friendship between the guys and then their families as marriage and parenting ensued. Myself, Joanne, Sara and Alisa; David, Andrea, Jesse and Seth have been connected throughout life's various roller-coaster rides.

I am confident that there is much written in his memoir about David's life and career and his myriad contributions to individuals, the community, and the world at large through his professional work and his many acts of kindness and generosity.

My main comment is that David was the best listener in the world. His authenticity and genuine interest in the person across from him always resonated with the other person.

I watched with amazement some of the probing conversations he had with each of my daughters during various ages and stages of each girl's own development. Thanks to his totally open and non-judgmental style, our daughters would open their hearts and minds to David in ways that they didn't with other adults or even their parents.

His encouragement, his advice, and his caring were well received, and David became the "additional Dad by choice" of our children. David officiated our daughter Sara's wedding in France (her husband is French) in October, 2018 — a truly bilingual celebration, at a time that we were also so appreciative that David still had an active and joyful life while managing his illness.

Rabbi Nossen Schafer, Chaplain and Friend: I'd already been working for a few decades as a chaplain visiting Jewish patients in Rhode Island hospitals when, five years ago, I looked down the list of new patients. When I entered one room the man in the bed appeared very emotional. When I asked him what was going on, he said he had just learned he had a terminal illness. I sat with him and he shared his feelings with me. I sang some of Shlomo Carlebach's emotional *niggunim* (songs) and I could tell he appreciated it. I returned to him numerous times in the hospital, and after he was released I went to see him in his home numerous times. I was so impressed by him, about how ill he was but still with such an amazing ability to understand and share his feelings with me. He was consistently open to me and to the deep discussions we were having — some in person, some on the telephone, during which he shared so much with me about his family and the work he'd been doing for a very long time. I began to understand this work as going into environments where people are radically opposed to each other's views, be they political or ethnic or military. Getting to know his deep caring and clarity and openness, I could tell why he'd been able to help people to see the point of the other's position, to help them step back from their fervent opposition. What have I learned from Dave Joseph? The importance of believing in people and helping them believe in each other and to see the goodness in the very same people they may have initially been very opposed to.

Amy Meisner Threet, Cousin: I really appreciated David's support while I was in social work school. When I failed the licensing exam by 3 points, David understood what a small margin that was. He encouraged me to try again, but due to my medical condition, I just didn't feel I could do it. David always acknowledged that I was a social worker and that meant so much to me.

Dilip Kulkarni, Friend and Supporter:
Reflecting on the Influence of Dave Joseph…

Before I share my reflections, I would like to suggest that families of individuals like Dave sacrifice to let them do what they do for communities and humanity. Therefore, Andrea, Seth, and Jesse, thank you for sharing Dave with us.

I wondered what I could say to express my experiences with Dave, especially since I had never worked with him. So, I will start by sharing the differences between Dave and me.

So let me share with you that I am not an easygoing person; people including Ruth, my wife, tell me that I love conflicts. I enjoy making people uncomfortable. I am judgmental. So, now you know that I am nothing like Dave. Maybe a total opposite.

So having Dave in my life was an unusual gift I was lucky to have. As I am not a peacebuilder, I did not work with Dave. So, my experience with Dave is probably different from most of yours. However, I suggest that our experiences with him were all founded in his ability to listen without being judgmental and to make us comfortable being us.

The first time I met Dave was at the MBBI conference in Baltimore. I wanted to share with someone at the MBBI my blunt thoughts about the MBBI. I was told to share my thoughts with Dave. I think that Ginny Morrison was there too. Dave listened and seemed to have appreciated my input. From that conversation, I knew that I could learn from him.

I recall my first conversation with Dave. I told him that I don't have conversations with someone I don't know. This means I don't have conversations with the public. So, what is the Public Conversation's Project? He smiled and quietly asked me how I got to know someone without having the first conversation. He asked whether I was not interested in knowing a person I did not know and what he/she thinks ... I got the message.

Now, I will share his influence on me for the last twelve years. We had conversations every three months about my educational journey and my interest in just communities, dear to Dave's heart. He was the kind of advisor who did not advise. When I shared my provocative thoughts, he would say, "interesting, would you please tell me more?" By the end of our conversation, I was not as provocative. Through our conversations, I learned to be more patient, thoughtful, and less judgmental.

After I shared my conversations with Dave with Ruth, who was a social worker, she would always say to me, "We need Dave, the world needs more Daves, more social workers to help you and the world."

I must confess that Dave is the only one I knew who could have a self-proclaimed harem and go with beautiful and intelligent women all over the world. Andrea, I don't know whether Ruth would have done that.

I am not a religious person. I have difficulties with the concept of God. However, I think that we experience God through others who accept us as we are with dignity, respect, and compassion; Dave did that for me.

So now, I am wondering what and how I can continue Dave's attributes and legacy. I am afraid that I may rely on saying, "Dave was one of a kind." However, I hope that I will keep on trying. I will keep on wondering how we can help in building peace without having peace in ourselves. I will try to finish my dissertation about how educational institutions can work with communities to help them become more just communities. I hope to dedicate this dissertation to my mentor, Dave Joseph. Dave gave us a gift, Andrea. Thank you for letting me share my reflections.

Claudia Gorbman, Friend: Andrea is one of my two oldest friends in the world — from 7th grade, 1960. She lives on the east coast, and I on the west. Her David, whom I had never met, was going to be in Seattle for a couple of days of work. It was a busy time — weren't we all forever caught up in the details of working life? I was mildly put out at the prospect of driving across the city and meeting someone I didn't know, though I was indeed curious about the person dear Andrea had raised her family with (and incidentally, about their email handle "malam dauda").

I hardly need tell you the rest. At dinner I bet I started out with small talk, which he was perfectly proficient in, but that didn't last long. He asked all about what I do, what I find important and meaningful. I asked him back. His curiosity for people, his passion to understand and connect, his humor and his desire to dive in, probably explain why I can't remember if we were eating Indian or Thai. I do remember coming home to Pam enthralled, exclaiming about this guy who gets people together to talk and resolve their differences. What a life path to have chosen, and what a lovely, evolved human to tread it and share it.

Andrea, I'm so glad for the love you found. If we do go on somehow after the last breath, you're in beautiful company.

MESSAGES AND MEMORIES FROM ASSOCIATES

Imam Muhammad Sani Isah, Intervention Director, Interfaith Mediation Centre, Nigeria: A Special and Sincere Tribute to My Revered Mentor Dave Joseph

I came into contact with Dave Joseph in the city of Kaduna, Nigeria over a decade ago. And I knew him in the company of Prof. Darren Kew, Seth Karamage and Ginny Morrison (known among us as Jameelah).

They trained us, with Dave as the lead facilitator, on reflective structured dialogue (RSD) techniques. When I say they trained us, I am referring to the officials and staff of Interfaith Mediation Center (IMC) Kaduna.

On many occasions, with some trainees under us, Dave made us put into practice what we learned from him about RSD, and we used it to train others under his supervision in the city of Bauchi in Nigeria.

Dave (popularly known among us as Malam Dauda) is a singular and a unique personality in terms of being humble, level-headed, being an exemplary leader and an upright mentor! He changed many of us, and I am one of them, from being judgmental, and harsh in conversation, or in asking questions, to becoming simple, polite, and constructive, even if one must criticize the other or an issue!

Whenever one of us slips out of the good practice, and offends someone in conversation, in asking questions, or in airing of an opinion; one will quickly apologize by saying: "Intention and Impact; I don't mean to hurt, and please pardon me!"

Malam Dauda (Dave) has never looked down on a person, has never belittled or underrated a contribution, or an opinion of someone!

He sees you as a human being first and last, and has never paid attention to your racial, ethnic, religious, cultural, geographic, social, economic, political, or any affiliation or status. And that's why he loved all, and all loved him!

He left behind a unique legacy in many documents and teachings, on how the RSD techniques can heal this our ailing world and build peace if taken seriously.

One of the documents Dave left is a book for which he served as an editor-in-chief in 2014. The book, Reflective Structured Dialogue: A Dialogic Approach to Peacebuilding, created by the Interfaith Mediation Centre, Public Conversations Project, University of Massachusetts Boston, and Collaboration Specialists, is unique for its contributions from both Christian and Islamic leaders.

Ginny Morrison, Owner, Collaboration Specialists: I've known Dave for more than 14 years. I live in Northampton and my work is improving mental health services in prisons. For years I was involved half in the prison work and the other half working internationally to help postwar communities rebuild their sense of community with each other. Dave and I attended each other's weeklong workshops and saw we were kindred spirits. We began looking for opportunities to do projects together. Even within Dialogue there are different theories on what's meaningful and effective. I like to focus on things that matter. If we can get a security deposit back from a landlord it matters to the tenant, for example, but this is not where I want to put my energy.

Liberia was memorable, but if I had to pick, I'd say our best work together was in Nigeria, from 2012-2016. We were a part of a big, five-year USAID-funded project, working with an existing Nigerian nonprofit focusing on building interfaith understanding and collaboration. It was as dangerous as the US civil rights movement in the '60s. Some of the feelings between Christians and Muslims were easily triggered and easily escalated into including physical violence.

The Nigerian organization we were helping was incredibly brave to initiate this work. It was and continues to be led by two charismatic leaders, one from each side. They were the kind of peacebuilders who had figured it out ... but there were limits to what they knew how to do and they wanted to expand their skills, which is where Dave and I came in. We helped them to lead the kind of dialogue that would cultivate the ability to build relationship before you even get to discussing the conflict. We were able to help them understand trauma as part of the conflict, causing reactive behaviors that can manifest violently. We were also there to help build the leadership within this organization to help the organization survive once the current leaders retire. We went back and forth to Nigeria over those years of the project, which was primarily run by UMass in Boston in partnership with Essential Partners. Dave was EP staff, and I was a subcontractor.

One of his gifts to the world is his tremendous insight and heart. He's deeply interested in understanding whomever he's in conversation with — not in intellectually picking them apart. He's genuinely interested in listening to them to bring the conversations into deeper places than ordinary conversations ever go.

Natalie Russ, Associate, Essential Partners: One time, Dave and I got stuck in the Madison airport. Wandering around with time to kill we found an idle ping pong table. Neither of us were very good, nor did we keep score, but we played for hours. Thus began the long-running joke of who won that game. Since then, whenever we corresponded or got together, one of us would rag the other about their brutal defeat, how they must still be embarrassed to have lost so terribly, how there would be a rematch one day. I even created a 2nd place trophy with a plaque to memorialize that experience.

Although Dave was so often kidding around, it always felt wholeheartedly good-natured. Never a mean moment or a sharp edge. Whether he was laughing at a joke, thinking deeply on a project, doing the work with humility and love, or bringing us younger practitioners up in the practice, Dave always showed up in the most connected, earnest of ways. He was profoundly trustworthy, with the light and the dark of life.

While I never got to give him his trophy, I can hear his jovial laughter. He would have appreciated my efforts to make sure the "2nd" was prominent and sparkly, to soothe his bruised ego. Upon thanking him for making me the ping-pong champion I am today by losing so thoroughly, he would have made a crack about revisionist history, as he usually did. He would have understood that this was my way of marking what he meant to me, as a teacher, mentor, and friend. What better way to honor Dave than with a good-natured joke.

Prabha Sankaranarayan, President and CEO, Mediators Beyond Borders, International: "It is my honor to have known Dave for the last fourteen years during which time we worked together in the USA as well as in Liberia, Thailand, Romania, and Indonesia; and with peacebuilders from many more countries. I am proud to call Dave and Andrea my friends.

I will never forget the first conversation we had. It was 2008 and he was interested in joining the Liberia project. Dave and I spent 90 minutes together sharing our work and values. Dave's wonderful questions (yes, he is the master of the most wonderful, thought-provoking questions) led us into depths not often possible in a first conversation. As we spoke, we were both exploring the context and conditions; and any questions I may have had about Dave's ability to work in these settings were quickly answered with the clear recognition that his gift of time, expertise, and wisdom would be invaluable to the team and the project!

It was clear that we were both at a stage in our lives and in our careers where we wanted to spend our time wisely, doing meaningful work and not wasting a minute. His unending goodwill towards people and his no-nonsense approach, always laced with hints of humor, were important parts of the joy of working together. Dave worked with dignity and playfulness; with imagination, insight, and pragmatism.

The depth of his impact may be seen in the work of peacebuilders carrying forward his commitment after he worked with people from Northern Ireland, Greece, Germany, Nigeria, Liberia, Burundi, Thailand, Philippines, Indonesia, Nepal, Rwanda, Colombia, Australia, Canada, and the USA.

Dave's focus on resilience extended to his 'engagement' with a brain tumor (it was never a 'battle' in his lexicon), and he emerged as an amazing five-year survivor during which time he taught the rest of us about grace and compassion. He focused his last months on creating what he found meaningful — mentoring dialogue facilitators around the world through video, a book, and supporting a community of practice that will continue on through MBBI!

When you work with Dave you can tell that what he does is also who he is. He's totally devoted to healing, and with a quality of integrity and humility that has now, I hope, become a part of the organization. The events he designed, many of them gathering people from around the world, were all imbued with his spirit. Every one of them was deliberately designed to create opportunities for connections that would never have happened otherwise. The last congress in Bali will remain a memorable one thanks to Dave's contributions.

And on those occasions when we'd land in some desperate, very tense situation, I could not have asked for a better person to be there with. Dave was calm and patient but also totally focused on the best way to tackle the problem at hand. And I knew that we always had each other's backs, that we would work hard to regroup for the next day, and that at the end of the day, we could sit and laugh about it over a glass of Long Island iced tea — we've had them all over the world.

After taking his Power of Dialogue course through Essential Partners in 2010, even though we'd already worked together, I learned more about Dave's absolute devotion to peace-making and knew that this is really a spiritual practice we both shared.

One priceless moment: at a meeting of the women's project in Liberia, the woman leading it had to leave the country suddenly and all these men from the community came and started to run the meeting. A couple of us women told them that this is a project for and by women, but we got nowhere; they ignored us completely and proceeded to keep running the meeting. Until Dave began to speak, steadily and clearly and with authority. They listened and bowed completely to whatever he said. He simply knew that you have to go with what's going to make an impact — and at that moment it was as a male and an elder (he often used his gray hair to good advantage).

"Mind the gap," he used to say, "the gap between intent and impact." That's a Dave-ism, one of many I still have in my head. Coming from such different backgrounds, what bound us together? Values, values, values. Knowing what he knew about the conditions around the world, he never failed to honor people's lives, their feelings, and their resiliency, wherever and whoever they were. I was very fortunate to have these 14 years with him.

Steve Seeche, Community Mediator:
I remember talking with Dave about skills that ultimately become wisdom.

We spoke of asking clarifying questions which is a subset for me, of focusing on asking questions of "genuine curiosity" which for me, whether in dialogue or in mediation or in everyday life, is one of the richest ways to convey a sincere interest in another person, whether I am in dialogue or whether I am forging a deeper more meaningful connection or relationship or friendship.

I recall one of the trainings I attended that Dave led. And during the role-play phase he demonstrated a way to connect with a person with whom he was dialoguing into a deeper connection. I recall he asked the person what their vocation was. And they told him they were a realtor. And he replied that he believed he knew what a realtor does or is, but rather than assume he was correct in his understanding he would prefer to hear from them what it means for them to be a realtor and how it works for them. His question, which I would never had thought to ask if I had been in his place (because everybody "knows" what a realtor is) opened a rich conversation of sharing and giving and receiving.

What it taught me is that when we assume we know or understand the nuances of another person's life, we miss the opportunity not only to learn and see and hear but also the opportunity to offer our deepest interest and caring for who they are and to welcome the opportunity for them to give us a deeper gift of themselves. It moves us from the limits of superficial interaction to the possibility of profound connection. And it opens the possibility to explore how to transcend the typical limitations of words hindering the possibility to hear another person express their deepest truths and identity and values.

And this can open a deeper possibility to explore where seemingly differing values might not really be differences but rather be a difference merely in the way we express and explore and share and find truths we have in common. And so a seemingly simple opportunity to "ask" transforms assumed facts into a door to appreciation and sharing and understanding and validating and becomes an extraordinary and genuine possibility to enhance connection through dialogue. And this all happened for me experiencing Dave demonstrating the skill on how to open a door to another person's life to invite dialog. And that skill has become wisdom for me — the ability to become genuinely curious — a gift Dave gave to me which is a beautiful part of my love and admiration for him and our friendship and that which is enduring for me and enduring for others each time I retell this beautiful story of my dear friend Dave.

Mallam Abdullahi M. Sufi, Director of Research and Documentation at the Interfaith Mediation Center in Kaduna, Nigeria: It was a frightening and sad moment to read this message about our dear friend and mentor.

Mallam Dauda, as he wished us to call him during his facilitating session, because he was conversant with the Hausa language and experience with Hausa-speaking people for many years in Niger, is a man whom I hold in high estimation.

It does not matter how long one lived in this world but how well one lives in this transitory and temporary station called the world.

Mallam Dauda spent most of his precious life in the service of humanity, which according to my faith tradition a person with such moral behavior is described as the best among human beings as all men are the family of one God and the best amongst them is he who served his family best.

Mr. Dave has accomplished his mission and left an ever-perpetuating legacy that will live after him for generation after generation in the world of academia and peace making.

The impact of his work in producing students of Reflective Dialogue Structure is another fact and testimony that Mallam Dauda or Dave, dead or alive, will remain immortal and will equally remain blessed.

Dave and his family, associates, friends, fear and grieve not. Remain resolute, put your trust in God who is the giver and the taker and to Him belongs whatever there is in heaven and on earth.

There is no mortal being that is in heaven or on the earth but must have to return to God as a slave, bearing in mind that death is not the annihilation of man but a transition from a lowly stage of life to a higher stage of life that is better and more lasting.

So life is but a walking shadow. This world is not our home, but one we pass through like strangers or travelers.

Death is the end of a journey and the beginning of another as is a common lot destined to all creatures. Dave is an ethereal soul that never dies.

We meet to depart and we depart to meet.

ESSENTIAL PARTNERS

Remembering our Friend, Colleague, and Mentor David Joseph

John Sarrouf and Katie Hyten Co-Directors, Essential Partners
We are heartbroken to announce that our friend, colleague, and mentor Dave Joseph passed away on October 25. His wife, Andrea, was by his side.

A leader in the field of peace-building, mediation, and dialogue for more than thirty years, Dave Joseph joined Essential Partners (then known as the Public Conversations Project) in 1996 as a facilitator of dialogue about abortion policy, and served in several capacities until his passing. During his influential tenure with EP, he was a mentor, a teacher, and an innovative practitioner. He touched countless lives and made healing possible in hundreds of communities around the globe. He embodied the teaching of his faith to pursue *Tikkun Olam* — to repair the world. The impact of his work cannot be measured.

"Dave was a shining light for dialogue, peace, and reconciliation whose work resonates around the world," said longtime colleague Bob Stains. "He inspired me, taught me, and was an amazing model of a husband, a father, and a person who lived a dialogic life."

Dave was raised in Buffalo with a deep sensitivity to the injustices of the world around him. After college he joined the Peace Corps in Niger, a formative experience. Dave returned as a teacher at an innovative school before studying at Smith College to become a clinical social worker. He worked for two decades in mental health and addictions programs before training as a mediator and founding the Center for Mediation & Collaboration in Rhode Island (CMCRI). He was a founding member of Mediators Beyond Borders and served as its Board Chair for many years.

For thirteen years, Dave served as our Director of Programs, and was both an expert practitioner and an invaluable mentor. His work with Essential Partners took him across the United States and throughout the world, bringing his skills to countries including Nigeria, to promote interfaith dialogue, and Liberia, for significant post-civil war projects, as well as to Burundi, for work in post-genocide healing. Dave walked with humility and hope into deeply polarized communities and post-conflict regions; he was deeply committed to supporting each unique group as they shepherded families, former combatants, and victims into new lives together. He returned from Liberia with a memento of the "Palaver (talking) huts" — bullet casings turned into tiny sculptures of huts used for resolving disputes — which he gave away as gifts. Many of those who were mentored, trained, and tutored by Dave now possess one of these sculptures, a small but powerful reminder of the transformational power of our work.

For so many of those who practice the work of dialogue, Dave's generosity opened the door to this world of peace-making and bridge-building. He would invite his junior colleagues to join him at conferences, brown-bag lunches, and workshops. He spoke in classrooms across the country. His vision for this work spanned generations, because he understood how deep the fissures are that divide us. That same imaginative vision allowed Dave to innovate important and powerful dialogue tools, which are used today by tens of thousands of communities on every inhabited continent.

In his personal life, Dave managed to surpass even the generosity he showed in his work. He, his wife Andrea, and their sons welcomed peacemakers from around the world into their lives and homes, embracing them as extended family. He could talk football with anyone, splitting his allegiance between his hometown Buffalo Bills and his adopted New England Patriots. He would take friends and colleagues rock climbing—a guy in his sixties and seventies putting mentees in their twenties to the test—his snow-white curls bouncing up and down as he scaled the wall. Everyone at his climbing gym loved him. Even as he faced illness, he would walk five miles each morning to maintain his strength.

He leaves us in grief and celebration of a life well lived—with a difficult situation he would term an AFGO*. It is difficult to imagine a future without him. We become the grateful bearers of his legacy, a life of service and compassion, a passion for justice, a commitment to peace. He will remain with us, heart and soul, and his work will continue to live through us.

Another F#%ing Growth Opportunity

MEDIATORS BEYOND BORDERS INTERNATIONAL

Celebrating the Life of a Great Man:

Dave began his work as an educator and a social worker. These early callings, along with his heart connection with West Africa, that began with Peace Corps work in Niger, shaped the rest of his professional life. He emphasized the power of dialogue to restore relationships, and mentored practitioners to fully develop their talents in order to ensure a sustained, vibrant dialogue field.

Dave's impact on MBBI is deep and wide. He initially joined the MBBI Liberian Initiative, focused on integrating women of nine ethnic groups who fought in the civil war, or who were stolen as sex slaves, with the community in which they were abandoned. He shaped MBBI's growth and relationships while serving on committees, as a board member, and as the Chair of the Board of Directors. He led strategic planning efforts at critical stages of the organization's growth including the latest one — the most inclusive and transformative process for MBBI so far. MBBI's International Conferences were enriched by his extraordinary design skills as we created spaces for what "we must discover together as we deepen our trust and understanding of the other."

Dave worked with dignity and playfulness, with imagination, insight, and pragmatism. He was a true servant leader. The depth of his impact may be seen in the work of peacebuilders carrying forward his commitment after he worked with people from Northern Ireland, Greece, Germany, Nigeria, Liberia, Burundi,

Thailand, the Philippines, Indonesia, Nepal, Rwanda, Colombia, Australia, Canada, and the USA.

Dave's focus on resilience extended to his 'engagement' with a brain tumor (it was never a battle in his lexicon), and he emerged as an amazing five-year survivor during which time he taught the rest of us about grace and compassion. He focused his last months on creating what he found meaningful: mentoring dialogue facilitators around the world through video, this book, and supporting a community of practice that will continue on through MBBI!

We will miss him deeply. We will honor him and celebrate his extraordinary gifts. We invite you to join us in carrying his legacy of love and care for the world through your work and through your support of the organizations for which he cared deeply.

THE GENTLE POWER OF DAVE JOSEPH, DIALOGUE LEGEND

**Tribute to a Friend, Teacher,
and Mentor to Many Young Dialogue Practitioners,
Including Myself**
*As appeared in the online magazine Public Square,
November 16, 2021, reprinted by permission*

By Jacob Hess PH.D, Executive Director of the Council for Sustainable Healing, served on the board of the National Coalition of Dialogue and Deliberation.

I was a little nervous when I walked into the 2006 gathering of The National Coalition of Dialogue & Deliberation. As a conservative kid from Utah, I wasn't exactly the type of person flocking to a convening like this. I wondered, would I even belong here?

But then ... I met Dave. Passing by the Public Conversations Project booth (now Essential Partners), I encountered someone who answered that question for me definitively. The French philosopher Emmanuel Levinas, of Lithuanian Jewish ancestry, taught that truth comes through the "face of the other." In the face of Dave (and others in the dialogue and deliberation community), the truth became very apparent. I did belong here. We all do ... or at least, we all can.

Beyond Dave's gentle personal way alone, the specific approach he represented with Essential Partners was especially reassuring for the way it made clear space for ideological diversity -- exactly the point unclear to conservatives (and others) in our cancel-happy-culture today. Over the years, the distinctive power of the Reflective Structured Dialogue approach advanced by Essential Partners has become widely appreciated as their workshops became standing-room-only affairs. (As a mindfulness teacher, I sometimes tell others that Essential Partners trainings are for Dialogue what the University of Massachusetts Center for Mindfulness is for meditation: the gold standard.)

Over the years, I kept going back to NCDD conferences and kept seeing Dave. When he came to Utah for another event, this inquisitive soul came over for dinner and met my family. We began talking about bringing the signature "Power of Dialogue" workshop to Utah. We talked about it so many times that it became an inside joke: "Yeah, one day!"

But then it happened! Several cohorts of Utahans came together in late 2017 and early 2018 - participating in this in-depth dialogue training with the express aim of cultivating a "practice network" of dialogue teachers in the region, similar to supportive networks available to mindfulness teachers wanting to hone their craft. The trainings definitely made an impact. Reflecting on her experience, participant Becky Linford said, "I think about what I learned every day and consider it an experience of a lifetime!"

This is only a subset of beneficiaries of the training in Utah - which, of course, is only one place impacted by his influence and teaching. And, as John Sarrouf, Co-Executive Director at Essential Partners, said at the memorial, "Nobody is more responsible for building the next generation of dialogue facilitators than Dave" — suggesting that his "students' students' students" can now speak of his impact.

The global impact of one determined peacemaker. After working for two decades in mental health and addictions programs, Dave spent the last 25 years of his life peacebuilding around the world. In his work with Essential Partners, he fostered interfaith dialogue in Nigeria and led projects in post-civil war healing in Liberia and post-genocide healing in Burundi. His legacy includes groups like the "National Ex-combatants Peacebuilding

Initiative" and Mediators Beyond Borders, of which he was a founding member and served as its Board Chair for many years. As one speaker at his memorial said, "You only have to listen to the people he worked with to know how much light he brought into dark places."

Dave did plenty of peacemaking work on home soil as well, supporting a wide spectrum of dialogues involving difficult questions, from abortion to immigration. He also founded the Center for Mediation & Collaboration in Rhode Island (CMCRI). His impact across the nation and around the world is obviously something to celebrate and honor. But I was especially touched at the memorial to see something not exactly common in people who make such a difference in the larger world — where those making a sizable impact in the larger world often leave broken families and unhappy home lives in their wake.

I knew better from Dave, who spoke of his grandchildren so frequently that I felt as if I knew them. The tender words of his closest family members and children during the memorial service left the biggest impression on me. Both sons spoke about celebrating the Patriots' improbable come-from-behind win in 2019 when they all went to the Super Bowl. And one son spoke of how his father had taught him the meaning of life, "centered on how one chooses to spend one's limited time on the planet": prioritizing "laughter, sharing wisdom, living with others, and living for the good of others." His other son said he had learned from his dad that "greatness is a measure of impact, not of value."

His sweetheart Andrea was at his side till the end, sending lovely updates to his many friends over the difficult months. As his obituary notes, "He and Andrea held hands until the end."

Remarking that Dave "lived his life hoping to help heal a broken world," Andrea added at his memorial that his "chief regrets" were not being able to spend "more time with his grandchildren and more time with his work."

Those at the receiving end of his attention were changed by it. Dave's sister described how he "always thought deeply and listened deeply ... listened really, really deeply" - commenting on how he "always helped me feel seen, heard, valued, and respected." John Sarrouf spoke of the striking "language" of his distinctive eyebrows when in conversation — reflecting "how closely he listened and considered what you had to share."

I was struck by how well Dave lived out two teachings he loved, both mentioned at the memorial service: "All real living is meeting" (Buber), and "I will destroy my enemies by converting them to my friends" (Maimonides).

Not just family members, of course, benefited from these gifts. I was touched by the stories of how famous he was at the climbing gym he frequented. "Not only because he was twice or three times older than other climbers — and not because he could climb the best routes — but because he invested so much of his time at the climbing gym in other people. He was not rushed, and asked people how their day was, getting to know the story of people's lives."

Three other qualities stood out from those reflecting on his life:

Patience. John Sarrouf described how Dave would "stand in the middle of people in the deepest of conflicts" and "pause in the most incredible, thoughtful, intentional way." Dave was described as "fiercely patient" — citing a proverb he often referenced in his teaching: "Patience is the medicine for everything in the world."

Humility. In reflecting on Dave's writing, John noted that he "never spoke about himself and his own wisdom and accomplishment, instead always focusing on someone else he helped to support." He added, "He was never the hero of his own stories. And was far more likely to tell you his failures and mistakes." His sons likewise spoke of how teaching from their father "rarely came directly," and instead through "asking questions." They both affirmed, "his wisdom was in helping others discover the wisdom for themselves."

Laughter. I absolutely loved Dave's laugh–look at the video to see why (https://www.youtube.com/watch?v=IFKz7o0sA9w&t=2201s&ab_channel=JacobZ.Hess]) One of Dave's sons described the "pure life and love when my dad laughed" — saying, "he laughed easily, wonderfully." The story was told how an hour after brain surgery — his head wrapped in gauze — he asked his family after waking up, "what do you think of my new look?" When one person at a workshop questioned the value of dialogue, Dave quipped, "Yes, this work of dialogue is only really useful for those who have to deal with other people."

I didn't know Dave at the depth of others who worked closely with him and loved him best. But as I reflect on the cumulative impact of my interactions with him over the years, I get emotional.

In hopes of preserving some of his wisdom for others to relish, I reached out to propose an interview four years ago. He agreed, and we found time in between Power of Dialogue events in Utah one evening in February 2018 in his hotel room (my excuse for some random background noises here and there!) I focused my questions on some of the lessons that had most impacted me and his reflections on his work over the years as a whole. I present in the video all of his answers, along with a few instances of back-and-forth where I was able to capture his unforgettable laugh. Hoping you enjoy it!

I found this comment of his, that we captured on the video, an especially powerful articulation of one challenge we will continue to face in the years ahead: "In times of polarization, what happens is the zealots get empowered — the voices that get heard are the most extreme. It's set up to create something we consume — that sells commercial products. People who are more complex and nuanced (which describes most Americans) aren't going to be the ones invited on the shows because they're not as entertaining — conflict entrepreneurs take advantage of this because it sells … and it works for them."

Then, Dave pivots to look forward with some hope, saying "We're challenged to be our better selves, to be the kind of people who help to heal a broken country, a country that has enormous potential if we can only make it so." Near the end of the interview Dave says, "I've been fortunate enough to have passed along some important values and beliefs that have motivated me to do what I've done. I hope I've been successful in communicating some of those values to others who can do this work when I'm no longer doing it." He is encouraged "to think that when I'm no longer doing this in five or ten years, that there will be people who will be carrying on."

It's true that Dave's legacy will live on in hearts and minds, and lives — young and old — all around the world. But that's not all that will live on. I write this tribute as both a Latter-day Saint, and as someone who has lost my mother, my brother, and many other dear ones in my life. Based on some sacred experiences confirming to me that my loved ones have not 'ceased to exist,' I quote the great movie Gladiator to simply say, "I will see you again…but not yet. Not yet."

We believe the "same sociality which exists among us here will exist among us there, only it will be coupled with eternal glory." I rejoice in knowing the beauty of friendship and family does not just suddenly evaporate after death. I feel like Joseph Smith, who once said, "If I have no expectation of seeing my father, mother, brothers, sisters, and friends again, my heart would burst in a moment, and I should go down to my grave. The expectation of seeing my friends in the morning of the resurrection cheers my soul and makes me bear up against the evils of life."

These are tough times in our country and the world — and by many indicators, they could get even tougher. The truths and teachings that guided Dave's life have never been more important, urgent, and needed. As we turn our faces to the future, may we be cheered by knowing of the goodness, kindness, and convictions of those who came before. And no matter what we have to navigate in the days ahead, let's hold onto the ideals that guided their lives — and live to make them proud.

Thank you, Dave. I love you. All who knew you will miss you sorely!

Tributes from Utah "Power of Dialogue" Alumni

"I had the honor of participating in a Power of Dialogue training with Dave in 2017. This training was instrumental in shaping the Community Conversations programming Utah Humanities offers throughout the state. Hundreds of people have gathered in person and virtually to find greater understanding and respect. We have held conversations on topics ranging from immigration to the opioid crisis and all are grounded in Dave's philosophy of respectful dialogue. His legacy lives on in every Community Conversation."
— *Jodi Graham, Executive Director, Utah Humanities*

"I clearly remember Dave sitting in the middle of our circle demonstrating the power of questions. He posed a problem he was trying to work out and we were each to think of questions to help him get to the root of the issue rather than offer suggestions or ask clarifying questions. It was a deeply impactful exercise that I have used in my own faith community, with my children and spouse and in my work crafting questions to enable dialogue.

Dave brought warmth, authenticity and humor to this critical work and I was amazed at the breadth of his work across the globe. I am grateful our paths intersected and can say with absolute sincerity that he changed me. I am privileged to create resources and foster dialogue across the country and carry the lessons learned from him with me in my daily work. Prayers and condolences to those who loved him best and feel the sting of grief right now."

— Becca Kearl,
Director of Programming, Living Room Conversations

"Dave had a firm grasp on bringing people together and a clear way to encourage us to understand human nature in a way to overcome differences. We have utilized his techniques to ensure we are able to balance many of the perspectives of the community in teaching and educating the diverse people we serve."

— Pamela Gee, Opera by Children Director,
Utah Festival Opera and Musical Theatre

"I am honored to have been trained in dialogue by Dave Joseph, but he taught me far more than the art of facilitating dialogue. He taught me how to listen, how to learn, how to sit patiently with discomfort, and how to care. I can't imagine a man more gifted in not only teaching dialogue but in demonstrating humanity with grace."

— Shelly Sawyer Jenson, Master Herbalist

"I have found as I get older that I appreciate anyone who comes into my life and leaves me with something new and wonderful. Dave is someone who introduced me to a new way of conversing with others and opening up my heart in a thoughtful way. He helped me become more willing to share and discuss hard things. When I bring what Dave brought to the table in any relationship, it softens everything. He hit at the core of knowing humanity. I mean truly knowing humanity and realizing that life is complex and we see only a few pieces to the puzzle of someone else's life. Getting to know, love, and understand others puts more pieces together so we can begin to see them a little clearer which makes a whole lot of room for love and kindness to fill in the missing pieces. That connection in a relationship gets filled with richness pretty darn quick. God undoubtedly smiles for all that Dave gave to us."

— *Emily Allen, Master Mother*

"Dave was first and foremost a warm and beautiful human. The creases on his face bespoke a thoughtfulness and care come from much tilling the soil of understanding and compassion among enemies. His personal stories of patient prepping illustrated the importance of learning and appreciating where people come by their strongly held positions. His method of intent listening and then sitting for a few moments to really consider and reflect what another said still instructs and benefits me. Such lessons as he demonstrated and taught continue to seed and grow a greater capacity for reconciliation for me and many others as we work to create a less divisive world. I mourn his passing."

— *Jay Griffith*

"Dave Joseph helped me take my interest in deep listening and become a leader. When I met him, I was trying to figure out how to use my voice — to use the tools of audio journalism to help people navigate fractured times and take courageous steps toward connection. Shortly after I attended a training with Dave, I developed a podcast about how to connect in a time of division. It was called Next Door Strangers and I produced it in partnership with public radio station KUER. NPR selected an episode for national promotion on their app and it reached more than 200,000 listeners. The podcast also got more people involved in the kind of dialogues that Dave champions by partnering with Living Room Conversations. I know that Dave — in his devotion to this work — has planted many seeds that are still developing."

— Andrea Smardon, journalist and podcast producer

"Dave really made me think. His example of patience and non-judgment towards others kept my own beliefs in check. Just recently I was able to use skills I learned from him in managing some tense workplace issues. Whether it was as a mediator, counseling soldiers, or listening to a friend, Dave's example will always be in my mind and in my heart."

— Andrew Evans

"This sad news of Dave's passing has reached me. The gifts of dialogue that Dave brought to me and many others have forever changed the way I think and the way I speak. Because of Dave Joseph, my goal is always, now, to find 'the heart of the matter.' I am just very fortunate in doors continuing to open for advocating and speaking out for social justice and protection of those marginalized by our government, legal, religious, and social systems. The work of Essential Partners is pivotal to every conversation in my life."

— Ashtora

Undated: *Yes, I love what I do!*

EPILOGUE
BY ANDREA JOSEPH

Like just about everyone else in the sane world who had the option, David and I had been mostly hibernating since March of 2020, taking safety precautions when we did go out and learning to have a social life on Zoom, as we tried to avoid contracting the feared Covid-19 virus. We had traveled to Cuba in January with David's sisters and their husbands, and went on a family trip with Jesse, Seth, and Jodie, and our four grandkids to Disney in late February, but since then had been hunkered down.

Then, in early October, 2020, David noticed some distressing symptoms reminiscent of four and a half years earlier when he was first diagnosed with glioblastoma multiforme (GBM is a terminal brain tumor). GBM took the lives of Ted Kennedy, John McCain, and Beau Biden, among thousands of others who typically succumb within twelve to fourteen months.

His original tumor was in the right parietal lobe, affecting the area of the brain that controls motor functions on the left. In late March of 2016, he noticed he couldn't tie the knots in his climbing rope. As a long-time rock climber, it was something he should have been able to do with his eyes closed. My first thought was that he'd had a stroke. His primary care doctor arranged for an MRI. When he called on April 1, 2016 with the results, our lives were irreparably changed.

After receiving the standard of care (SOC: surgery, radiation and chemotherapy) David was incredibly — amazingly — fortunate that all symptoms disappeared. His approach to his situation was that he was living with cancer, not dying from it. That said, knowing that the tumor could and would return at any moment, we turned our energies to living life as fully as possible. David returned to his work, as did I to mine: he went back to rock climbing; we traveled extensively, and spent as much time as possible with our families and especially our grandkids and my dad, who had just turned 100 that year.

Over the course of the next four years I almost forgot that the other shoe was still hanging there, waiting to drop. But in October of 2020, David couldn't get his left fingers to hit the correct letters on the keyboard. An MRI confirmed that the tumor was back and had spread. Very quickly he lost the ability to use his left hand and arm, and his left leg started to drag. Surgery was not an option this time around, but he endured five weeks of daily radiation and concurrent chemo — that is, until early December when he was diagnosed with Covid-19. At that point he had to go off the chemo, but continued radiation. Covid knocked him out even more than the radiation/chemo, but we managed to keep him out of the hospital … until towards the end of the virus, when he developed a very large blood clot in his left leg. Sending him off in an ambulance, unable to go with him because of Covid, it doesn't take much to imagine the devastation we felt.

Thankfully, he was placed on blood thinners, and I was able to bring him home the same day.

As the months passed, David had visits from a physical therapist to retain his strength, an occupational therapist to help him adapt to the loss of use of his left side, and a speech therapist to help him read. When those therapies failed, we just carried on as best we could, day-to-day-to-day, buoyed by the many visits and loving support of family, good friends, and colleagues/friends. The only thing we couldn't do was to stop the progression of the deadly tumor.

And so, the year 2021 got off to a rocky start and went downhill from there. The world went from rapture that Covid was going away, to dismay and disbelief that it was roaring back. We had started to adapt to David's new status with an active tumor and the damaging effects of radiation necrosis, and we hunkered down again.

However, amidst the gloom, thanks to Prabha Sankarnaranayan, Veronica Jacobs, and Ben Lutz at MBBI, David was encouraged to start a Zoom based community of practice. During monthly *"Dialogues with Dave,"* members of the next generation of practitioners from around the world whom David had trained gathered to share their experiences and learn from each other: specifically, what worked, what didn't, and how they had adapted their training to meet the needs of the communities with which they were working.

He repeatedly made the time — often pushing himself beyond his limits of strength and concentration — to speak at length with

Deborah Fineblum, his ghostwriter. Thanks to his courage in doing so, this memoir was made possible. We hope it will continue to provide everyone who reads it with the insights, inspiration, and encouragement to be the kind of peacemaker David was.

I am eternally grateful to our sons Jesse and Seth for their love and constancy. Seth, who lives locally, decided to work from our house every Friday so I could get out to run errands, and so he could help me with household chores that required more brawn than brains! But really, he highly valued that precious time to spend being and talking with his dad. And our daughter-in-law Jodie supported Seth running over whenever I needed his help! Our regular Sunday brunches with them and our grandkids Stella and Pierce were a source of great comfort. Jesse, who lives in Virginia, called often and video chatted with us regularly so we could see and talk with his kids, our grandsons Alex and Davey. They also visited several times — guaranteed to cheer us up — and Jesse came up on his own as often as he could to be with us. I love you both beyond words.

David's sisters Judy and Ruthie were wonderful, loving, and supportive throughout this ordeal, and we remain very close. Ruth, a physical therapist, flew out from Albuquerque numerous times to help us learn new ways to accommodate David's changing needs, bringing her warmth and humor along with her professional skills. Judy visited often from Columbus, offering her own brand of humor and always good advice. She has been a steady friend to me as well.

We were blessed to have found Kerri, a wonderful private CNA with whom David became very close. She quickly became essential for her warm personality, excellent care, intelligence and willingness to help out with any chore. David and Kerri spent hours talking while I was out running errands or having a lunch break with a friend.

There are so many people who helped make the unbearable almost bearable. Their care and concern, humor and good conversation always lifted our spirits. Marc and Joanne Jacobs, among our oldest friends, held vigil with me in the hospital back in '16 and have been by our sides throughout. Longtime friend Carol Peckins, with her son (and our godson) Joshua and his lovely wife Lilit, came down from Massachusetts bearing Carol's always delicious meals and Lilit's awesome baked goods. David's cousin Jonathan and his wife Paula (who has become my friend) came frequently and got us addicted to the food and pastries from their favorite Cambridge bakery. His other cousins Marc, Todd, Neil, and Bruce, with their respective wives Brooke, Barbara, Katrina and Shirley, all visited, as did my brother Joel. Old friends Bob Gould and Wendy Costa brought lunch and good company and tales of travel. David had made a special connection with a newer friend of mine, Lucette Nadle, and she and her husband Barry Kran made the drive down several times to spend time with us bringing wholesome treats. Michael (David's best friend) and Ellie Kaplan came from Indiana to share their love, warmth, good food, and good cheer. Local dear friends Barbara Kahn and Doug Counts brought goodies from their garden. Other friends who supported us with wonderful visits included Marsha Rice and Craig Kercheval, and Dan Even. There's a theme here — pretty much everyone brought food! And it was always appreciated.

So many of David's beloved colleagues/friends — Ginny, Steve, Prabha and her husband Sankar, Mary Jo, Bob, John, Corky, Maggie, Kathy, Alison—came from near and far to be with him and us. Raye Rawls and Dilip Kulkarni weren't able to make it here but spoke with us often. Sallyann Roth and Carole Samworth sent frequent poignant messages and thoughtful gifts.

A special shout-out goes to Joan Coulon, another of David's nine cousins and one of my closest friends. We made a wonderful new memory that has become part of the family lore when Joanie, her husband John, and her visiting brother Bruce and his wife Shirley brought her parents, Uncle Dick and Aunt Marion, here to visit. We surprised her father with platters of buffalo wings (courtesy of Goldbelly.com) direct from Duff's Famous Wings - Dick's favorite buffalo wings joint. I don't know who enjoyed the event more - David or his uncle! Joanie schlepped here often from Lynn, Massachusetts to be by our sides, including during David's last days in hospice.

If I have omitted anyone I am truly sorry. We kept a calendar on a large whiteboard so David could see what was happening, and many visits did not make it from the whiteboard to my digital calendar (or my brain!).

Finally, I owe a great debt to the people who gave their time generously to help with the nuts and bolts of getting this book to print. My dear longtime friend Claudia Gorbman and my new friend Brucie Harvey - both writers extraordinaire – offered astute (and not overwhelming) suggestions. And Nicky Nichtern, a multi-talented fundraiser, artist, and graphic designer, whipped the text and pictures into this final product you are holding in your hands. David's nephew Vincent Valentino designed and produced the website www.malamdauda.com that will both promote the book and support David's passion for helping others in the field with resources.

A few months after the GBM returned, a palliative care doctor recommended that we consider completing the "Five Wishes." Like a living will, the Five Wishes provides the opportunity to make your desires known concerning your choices around treatment, but it goes beyond communicating with healthcare professionals and poses questions about your relationship with your faith, your family and your community, however you define that.

Here is what David wanted you to know:

"If anyone asks how I want to be remembered, please say the following about me:

"He lived his life working to help heal a broken world. He was fortunate to have met and married Andrea Bender with whom

he had Jesse and Seth. He could not be prouder of the men they have become and the fathers and partners they are."

He also said he wanted our memories of him to give us joy, but he accepted that his death will cause us to experience sorrow.

And David wanted you to know that he felt privileged to work with outstanding colleagues and friends at both Essential Partners and Mediators Beyond Borders in doing the work he was born to do. His chief regrets were that he would not have more time with his grandchildren, and he would not have more time for his work. Sadly, so sadly, David passed away on October 25, 2021.

His life had meaning, and his legacy lives on in his family, in everyone whose life he touched. David was heartened by the knowledge that the work of building peace which our world so sorely needs will, indeed, be carried on. His influence will continue to expand wherever he has worked. My hope, like David's, is that you, dear reader, will have found something, some spark, some bit of wisdom in the telling of his story that will help and inspire you, whether it be within your own family, your religious community, your work life - wherever.

Peace,
Andrea